Ocosingo War Diary:
Voices from Chiapas

Jan 2019

For my dear friend

Kent —

David.

OCOSINGO WAR DIARY

Voices from Chiapas

by Efraín Bartolomé

Translated from the Spanish by

Kevin Brown

CALYPSO EDITIONS

CALYPSO EDITIONS

www.CalypsoEditions.org

By unearthing literary gems from previous generations,
translating foreign writers into English with integrity,
and providing a space for talented new voices, Calypso
Editions is committed to publishing books that will endure
in both content and form. Our only criterion is excellence.

Front cover photo: Efraín Bartolomé
Back cover photo: Guadalupe Belmontes Stringel
Interior Illustration: Balam Bartolomé

Book layout & cover design: Golden Ratio Design
www.goldenratiodesign.anthonybonds.com

ISBN 13: 978-0-9887903-3-9

First edition, June 2014
Printed in the United States

for my son, Camilo Brown-Pinilla,
who's been teaching me how to be a father;
and for his mom, Martha Lucia Pinilla,
who's been teaching me how to speak a little Spanish

TABLE OF CONTENTS

ACKNOWLEDGMENTS

Portions of this book originally appeared, more or less altered, in *Apuntes, Asymptote, The Brooklyn Rail, eXchanges, Hayden's Ferry Review, KiN, Mayday, Metamorphoses, Ozone Park* and *Two Lines*.

WAR DIARY

I was born in Ocosingo's first valley, when my village was still gateway to the jungle, and the jungle was still worthy of its name. In that atmosphere of pain and wonder you could plumb the depths of nature and human nature. In that smithy my soul was forged. There, in the old family house, the war took us by surprise. I kept a hasty record of what I saw and heard during those first 12 fateful days. The very valley that gave rise to my verse has also generated the snapshots which, in brushstrokes of stuttering prose, I transcribe below.

—Efraín Bartolomé

I JANUARY[1]

It's 8:57 on January 1, 1994.

My father wakes me with the news: "The town is taken over. The Zapatista Army of National Liberation has declared war on Salinas."

Incredulousness.

I stand up.

Get dressed.

My wife turns on the radio: nothing, except the local station converted to *Radio Zapata*, where a man with a Central American accent reads the Declaration of War upon the Mexican Army.

Total silence blankets the town.

My father affirms that the guerrillas already passed through the street "armed with high quality submachine guns."

The Declaration of the Lacandon Jungle continues to be heard.

I don't believe what I'm hearing.

I'm still not fully awake.

What's this.

The final "l" trills long on the palate of this revolutionary radio announcer when he says: *Ejército Zapatista de Liberación National-l-l-l.*

9:12 We're in a second-floor bedroom.

We've slept here during our vacation.

We go to the terrace overlooking the street and see, with the binoculars, a man in blue on the roof of town hall.

The *Internationale* is heard over the radio in an unrecognizable language.[2]

Russian?

The short station breaks are full of the "guerrilla" muzak we suffered through during the 70s.

9:17 My niece Teté, 9 years old, runs upstairs and tells me an armed group is coming past Arístides' house, on the corner.

I go out the medical office door and see a small group coming down the street, 10 or 12, and another group on the corner.

The shooting starts around the town hall building.

Isolated bursts of machine-gun fire and gun shots.

The War Tax Act begins to be heard.

My initial belief about the taking of the town as a harmless blow begins crumbling to pieces: an image comes to mind of the university "islands" of '71; fiery speeches, ultra-leftist thugs, the University President's fall, radical activists like Falcón, Castro Bustos and Raúl León de la Selva, sound systems at full blast electrifying the air with firecrackers.[3]

War Tax Act.

"They're repeating it over and over," says my brother-in-law Genner.

More gunshots.

A man in a little black hat, with a high-caliber weapon and impressive radio equipment, opens with a burst of machine-gun fire from the corner.

What's he shooting at?

They're barricaded on the corner down the street, outside my cousin Lety's house.

There're about seven of them.

Seems they're on both sides of the street.

Something explodes and makes smoke near the school.

Of course: that's what they're shooting at.

They're the State Judicial Police offices.

How quiet it is.

9:21 Some smoke from the explosion gets through. It burns the nostrils and makes your eyes water.

9:23 There're three radios on in the house, and yet the silence in the rest of town is striking.

This was the silence I used to hear as a child.

Severe watering of the eyes.
I look out from the garden terrace.
The odor and watering of the eyes increase.
I run downstairs.
My wife indicates they should give the children cloths soaked in water and vinegar so they can cover their noses.
There're eight children in the house.
They're all blinking with watery and startled eyes.

9:30 Now I look out from the terrace overlooking the street: the small group's still there, but the man with the antenna is no longer there. Two shots.

9:32 A new explosion and burst of smoke near the church. Naturally: the boys in blue from Public Safety, State Police, are protecting town hall.
They're the ones firing tear gas.

9:36 Ten more shots. The shootout continues. Five now. Now about 15, from different parts of town.

9:45 Just what we needed: José de Molina on Ocosingo radio.[4] I never thought that in this air so clean...
"That background music's gonna lose them the war," slips in my wife Guadalupe-Pilla-Pillis-Pillita-Pita-Pía-Pi, whispering.[5]
"It's one of two things: either the naturally bad taste of all wars or their most potent weapon for scaring off the enemy," I respond.
Why've we been whispering?

9:47 Another burst of machine-gun fire.
A truck suddenly appeared up the street.
It's coming from the highway.
Tries to enter.
Onlookers gathered at the street entrance shout:

"What're you doing there, man?! Don't even *think* about coming in! There's a shootout!"

The truck stops, the driver talks to people.

He backs up and heads toward the Yajalón exit.

9:57 You can already see some civilians venturing out into the street, as if taking their first steps.

My cousins Mario and Ovidio arrive.

Signal us from the corner.

Come with their backs against the wall.

We open the entry gate for them and they quickly dart through.

They say there're more than a thousand guerrillas in town.

That they've already burned down Pemex's Geophysical installation and destroyed three small planes.[6]

My cousins live over by the airfield, in the low-lying part of town, towards the big river or Virgin River, which surrounds and delimits the population to the east.

(The river runs north to south and merges with the Jataté River, some seven or eight miles from town.)

10:00 We chat at the upper gate, which is the entrance to the palm-tree patio: full of cars during this vacation season in which all of us brothers and sisters come to spend the holidays with my parents.

At the rear of the patio is the area for removing the pulp from coffee beans, and the orchard with its limes, orange trees, coffee trees and pacaya palms.

Goose, duck, turkey and hen country.

And seven roosters for the holidays.

My father's glad: "Those Zapatistas sure are some tough turkeys, alright," is his catch phrase lately.

There're four guerrillas on the corner.

No: six.

Eight.

Seems to be more, but I can only see those.

Well armed.

Another subject arrives with a radio.

Many arrive: quickly cross the street.

Now it's clear to me: their objectives are town hall and the State Judicial Police offices.

They're going after them from all parts of town, judging by the gunshots.

"Yep," cousin Mario confirms, "all the shots are aimed at town hall. It's a sea of green down there with so many guerrillas." They invited Mario and Ovidio to join them.

"They're inviting everybody."

"Against the rich."

"Don't worry about weapons, we'll give them to you."

I see boots, green pants, sweaters or brown jackets.

Red bandanas around their necks.

Some are wearing black pants.

"Those who join will receive weapons immediately, but if you have them, even better, a guy who talks like a Salvadoran told us," Ovidio says. My cousins came all the way from their house on the other side of town to see how we were, and to wish us Happy New Year.

Happy New Year?

The man with the little black hat and the huge antenna reappears at the corner.

Pants and jacket: all black from head to toe.

And his red bandana around the neck.

People lean out from balconies, from doors, from windows.

Me, I already scouted all the look-out posts inside the house, and already looked out from the sidewalk.

Everybody's going around taking little steps to reclaim his or her space, to once again mark a territory abruptly confined to the house by the presence of arms. A block up the street, on the highway, there's a throng of onlookers, 30 or 40, standing in the middle of the street or sitting on the sidewalks. They're truck owners, or drivers, or passengers who'd be traveling to San Cristóbal or to Palenque today.

Our house is on Avenida Central.

Block and a half down the street is Cuauhtémoc Federal Elementary, my old school.

A block further away, town hall bordering, to the east, our civic center (the central park and the battered colonial plaza).

On the other side of the plaza, and delimiting its eastern boundary, the great church of San Jacinto de Polonia, which Friar Pedro Laurencio's Dominicans built in the 16th century.

Given the location of our house, at the higher elevations of the populated area, I have a bird's-eye view of the theatre of operations.

I've been peeking out from the large upper gate, through the door of my brother Edgar's medical office, through the little gate of the coffee patio and from the second-floor balconies.

Mario says they did serious damage to don Enrique Solórzano's house.

I watch a drunk pass by the corner, staggering, with his white cowboy hat on, shaking his head as if in disapproval.

He passes between the guerrillas as if it were nothing.

He crosses the street, then comes back and continues up the street, in the direction of the school.

Now a gunfight breaks out.

Shots fired on town hall.

But it's not the ones on the corner who fired.

We don't budge from our observation post.

10:15 More tear gas near the State Judicial Police offices.

The drunk turns around at the school.

Three guerrillas come running to the corner.

They talk with the group that's been there.

Disappear.

I watch the man at town hall, a policeman in blue, in sniper position on the roof, underneath some satellite dishes.

He aims toward the park.

"There're several of them," my sister Aura says.

"There they are, look," and she passes me the binoculars.

"They're dragging themselves along the ground."

"Yeah, there they are; they're aiming toward the park: they have no weapons; they can only fire tear gas."

A guerrilla group appears at the corner of the school.

They take cover.
They're approaching town hall.
There they are now, a block away.

The war manifestos continue over the radio.

Throughout the hours we've heard a justification for the armed uprising, a war tax act, a series of petitions that international organizations like the Red Cross monitor combat developments, contribute to the care of the wounded and the burial of the dead. The declaration of war has been heard several times, as well as instructions for EZLN members, a series of rights and obligations of peoples in conflict in the "liberated" territories, and a series of rights and obligations for EZLN soldiers.

Respect for civilian populations is spoken of.

They invoke the Geneva Convention as to the conduct of war.

There shall be summary trials of policemen and soldiers who've received training abroad, charging them with treason against the homeland.

EZLN members who rob, kill or rape civilians shall be punished.

And the litany of revolutionary jargon goes on and on.

The echo of words like "summary trials," "executions," "battles," "war," "enemies of the revolution," "dead and wounded," produce an atmosphere of frigid silence.

10:22 Another group on the corner.

All very young, in their 20s or less.

These seem like college students: they all look completely ladino.[7]

There's one with a patchy little beard.

The ones from a while ago were clearly indigenous.

I no longer see the men on the roof at town hall.

10:24 They call me to eat breakfast.

The kitchen activities haven't been interrupted.

Every day of the year, very early, around seven o'clock, we drink coffee; then we work in the yards and in the orchard.

At 9 o'clock, we formally eat breakfast, at 2:30 we have lunch, and dinner is at 8:30 or 9.

The kitchen is in constant activity under my mother's vigilance.

I go down to eat breakfast and drink coffee but without letting go of my little notebook: this beautiful notebook, bound in amate paper, that the young poet Leonardo Cruz Parcero made.[8]

He wanted me to have that first product of his hands.

Thanks: I'll make these war diary entries here.

One of last night's turkeys was left almost whole.

Not bad for wartime: stuffed turkey with a flower in its beak.

Mini tostadas, salsas, home-grown coffee from our ranch and bread from San Cristóbal.

Let "rationing" be ever thus.

Yesterday and the day before rumors were running around: that armed men would come; "the Indians are going to take over the town"; "five Guatemalan planes came"; "the Indians are already ready in Monte Líbano."

Rumors.

"It'll be just like October 12th; nothing's going to happen."[9]

And a mock toast: "In case the guerrillas chop our heads off tomorrow."

To chop somebody's head off is an habitual turn of phrase in these valleys where the machete is both tool and weapon; the most useful, the first one learns to wield.

We all, as children, used to have the machete corresponding to our age and would use it for everything: for splitting pine wood, for chopping firewood, to make sticks out of and for making play pens, for making toy bows and arrows, for making wooden kite frames, for making stick-figure wooden horses, for chopping and stripping sugar cane.

I look at the machetes these guerrillas carry: small, with craftwork sheathes, toy-like, very uniform.

"They carry them like field knives," says cousin Pablo, who's attracted to military life.

To chop someone's head off.

To chop someone's head off.

To chop someone's head off...

No longer has the same ring to it as yesterday.

As if the words, now, had a sharp edge.

My aunt Maga proposes organizing medical brigades with the inhabitants of this house.

"Because it seems this is getting serious."

An expert in public health, recently retired from the IMSS, she now sells medical supplies.[10]

My brother Edgar, the youngest of the brothers, is this town's beloved doctor.

Our house has good mojo when it comes to medicine: my mother cured, always following the tradition my great grandmother inaugurated in the century's second decade, since the last war in this valley: the Pinedist revolt against Carranza.

My mother's oldest brother, uncle Ovidio, was, until his death, the most highly esteemed physician in San Cristóbal.

He used to come to Ocosingo twice a year, back when there was no highway.

And we would have long lines of patients stretching out to the street, sometimes all the way to the corner.

Rosario and Domingo, my sister Mapi's children, are studying medicine.

10:43 Four young drunks pass through the street, with their bottle of Jaguar, a sugar cane liquor bottled in plastic and costing a dollar per liter.

These drunks are part of a team of bricklayers famous for being "hard drinkers and hard workers."

"That one is el Pato," says my sister Aura, an architect; she knows them well.

"The other one is el Caracol, the one with his shirt open."

They were with the spectators up the street, and took off from there.

They arrive chatting.

Stop.

Take a swig from the bottle.

Pass it around.

Say something to each other.

Unexpectedly, after taking a swig and passing the bottle, the one with his shirt open turns toward the guerrillas on the corner and shouts at the top of his lungs: "Assholes! Kill me dead, *p-r-r-r-p-tow-tata-tow*; sons a fuckin' bitches! Think we're scared of you?!"

El Pato wants to run off up the street.

The rest stop him.

The armed men ignore the shouting.

These young people, with a bit of pressure, could join in on the violence of either side.

They go up, now, to the house of don Amado, the old carpenter. (When, as children, we would hear hammering at night, we knew that someone had died.)

There the drunks are now, lurching, with lost looks on their faces.

They talk.

Stick out their chests.

One lights a cigarette.

They're, really, very drunk: New Year's.

Three walk down again.

One stays back.

They call him: "Come on, dickhead."

Sporadic shots have been heard from the direction of the park. The exchange of gunfire grows more intense now.

One of the drunks, a curly-haired guy I don't know, screams, as if responding to the shoot-out: "Ow, ow, owww! "How life makes me laugh as long as passion lasts!"

They all light cigarettes.

Pluck up courage.

It surprises me, that almost animal posture of defiance that consists of sticking out their chests and walking, as straight as they can, in the midst of their drunkenness.

And there they go, back down the street.

The defiant ones.

There's a strange tension scorching the air of the street because of these youths whose only weapon is their bottle of Jaguar.

"Let's see what they do," says Genner.

They continue determined, down the street.

But at the corner they turn around.

"You're never too drunk to eat your own shit," adds my brother-in-law.

10:47 Fresh tear gas through the park.

We try calling Mexico City, and the call is cut off.

Rumor's been running around that telephone lines are tapped by the guerrillas.

Has it come to that?

Jaime passes through the street, with his yellow baseball cap on.

He takes care of the plot where we're building my house in Fortín del Chorro, in the eastern part of town.

That place was, indeed, one of four forts, during the siege of Ocosingo in the Pinedist war (from 1916 to 1920).

It's a privileged place for contemplating the valley.

"Jaime's happy now, thinking he's gonna get your house," says my sister Dora, smiling.

The drunken youths come back up the street again.

They've never passed beyond the corner.

El Caracol knows he's being observed: has onlookers from the store across the street, onlookers from the highway, and us, who see him from the terrace.

He turns around and shouts at the armed rebels again from the corner: "Put a bullet in me right here, see!"

And he violently thumps his hard bare chest.

"Suck my dick," he adds softly.

The spectators smile or titter.

Now it's the curly-haired guy who's carrying the bottle.
They have more trouble walking.
Continue up the street.
All of them.
The guerrillas aren't on the corner now.
Not visible at least.
Another drunk appears over there, alone.
Crosses the street.
Happy New Year!

11:02 Carmelino is the owner of "El Cubanito," the store across the street. With the curtains closed, he's selling to the few people who come bearing fresh news.

He reports that the guerrillas have don Enrique Solórzano, tied up.

His family, too.

"Poor Olga," my mother says, "what harm can Enrique have done them?"

"Bastards!" says aunt Maga.

"Weren't they going to respect civilians?" Dora adds.

They took their stuff and burned some of it.

They turned the prisoners loose.

They already killed three policemen from Public Safety.

They have the Solórzanos tied up and stripped down to their underwear.

"Looks like they're gonna kill 'em."

11:12 Over the radio they're repeating the Red Cross instructions.

Someone says it seems like a movie.

"Yes, but they're very slow; we want more action," says Oswaldo, an 11-year-old nephew.

11:29 Comments in the store:

"Nothing's known about the Mexican Army."

"Didn't there used to be a military detachment here?"

"We're so far from everything."

"It's an invasion."

"There're lots of Central Americans."

"Many of them don't talk."

"They're like Salvadorans."

"They're Guatemalans."

"They're Nicaraguans."

"But there're a lot of Indians from around here."

"From here?"

"Sure, the ones with rubber boots are from here, they were speaking Tzeltal."

"Some are carrying wooden rifles."

"There are women."

We're so far from everything.

It's true.

11:36 Past the corner a group of masked armed men passes.

Mario said a while ago that there were a lot like that, down there.

They're the first we've seen around here with their faces covered.

Ski masks or balaclavas.

A woman goes among them.

"Look how she walks, that one."

"It's a guy!"

"No, it's a woman, look at her hair."

Yes... seems like a woman.

11:39 Silence.

Short burst of machine-gun fire.

Isolated shots.

11:40 Mexico City television broadcasts the news.

They don't say anything about the shooting that's continued non-stop all these hours, albeit sporadic.

Minimal news: "a group of peasants armed with clubs is taking over San Cristóbal city hall."

They know nothing.

The sun burns, despite the cloudy day.

Birds' song accompanies the shooting.

Whistling, close by, a bullet.
Where from?

11:55 Another brief burst of machine-gun fire.

11:58 Two girls pass by the corner, between the armed men.
People get used to everything.
A kind of calm has descended.
Inside the houses I can manage to see, with the naked eye or with binoculars, people do laundry, prepare food, some sweep.
I watch the group of armed men on the school corner.
Big red stains of bandana against the light-colored wall.
I see the group on Lety's corner.
"Today we say, 'enough'!"
So begins the Declaration of War against the "dictator."
At times the voice of the man who's reading changes.
How many are there, I wonder?
Again, I see the men in blue on the roof of town hall.
Two Zapatistas cross the street, at the corner: one a girl with her face uncovered; the other, a male, ski-masked.

12:32 We're on the terrace overlooking the street.
My sister Aura, my wife, my cousin Pablo, my brother-in-law Luis.
We see the group from the corner and the one from the school.
Aura says: "Look... now they climbed up on the school roof!"
"Where?"
"There, near the heap of roof tiles!"
Yes, there they are.
There, up top, the guerrilla commando has in his sights the men in blue guarding town hall.
From rooftop to rooftop, but the policemen have their backs turned, looking towards the park.
We see the policeman in blue under the satellite dishes.
"They've got a potshot from the front," says Luis.

"They've got a potshot from the back," someone says.

"They're aiming at him!"

"They're gonna shoot at him!"

"No!"

"Yes!"

The shot rings out.

Man in blue slumps beneath the satellite dish.

Stupefaction.

Did you see that?

We've seen it so many times on TV; and now, faced with the real thing, we're trembling.

We look at one another, incredulous.

We're behind the walls under construction.

What time did we hole ourselves up here?

We were on the terrace unprotected looking toward the street.

They made us feel like yelling when they aimed.

"But if you yell they shoot at you, for sure."

We took shelter in the part under construction, behind the terrace, without realizing.

From here I watch and write, protected by a wall.

The blues move swiftly on town hall's rooftop.

As if they were lowering themselves on one side or another.

12:38 The commandos now have the State Judicial Police between a rock and a hard place.

We see them from the medical office door.

The group barricaded on Lety's corner fires in an orderly fashion: the first in line takes position with a knee to the ground, aims, fires, and goes to the rear.

The second does the same.

And so on, until they all go through. The ones from the school do the same.

"And those State Judicial Police, aren't they some tough hombres?" says my father, instigating.

"Come on out now and fight instead of holing up in there! Or let them remember when they kicked el Martín to death."

(El Martín came to Ocosingo at about the age of 9.

He'd fled his house near Tenango and came to live in town doing errands and working as a porter, shoe shine boy, chewing-gum street vendor.

When the highway arrived and the *Lacandonia* buses entered town, in 1971, el Martín became a freight loader.

One time a crate of tomatoes fell on him and severely injured his spinal column.

For a long time he couldn't walk, and the townspeople made him a wagon in which he went around followed by a throng of working kids whom he commanded with surprising leadership ability.

Here goes one scene:

"We're gonna climb the steep hill, you bastards! Everybody's gonna pull?," el Martín asked.

"Yeah-ah!, shouted the gaggle of kids.

"Well alrighty, then, sons of bitches! Some in front and the others in back! ¡On the count of three, push and pull! Fuck whoever doesn't pull, and mother fuck whoever doesn't push!"

And the wagon quickly climbed the steep ascent of Avenida Central amidst *yo momma* jokes, shouts and guffaws.

The kids used to bring him food, ran errands for him, lit his cigarettes, would go get his bottle of booze.

He started walking again, but the injury to his spine deformed him.

From then on, new generations knew him as el Martín the Hunchback.

My children, still young, met him on one of the town streets: perfectly drunk and dancing *El zancudito loco*.

One of the those travels about town they gave me the news: because of a robbery incident somewhere, the State Judicial Police arrested el Martín.

They beat him so severely that they killed him.

Left him lying near the highway, wrapped up in an old blanket.)

"Yeah, but those were some other guys. They ran them off a long time ago," my mother responds.

"No, those goddamned people are all alike," my father counter-attacks.

12:43 People get used to everything: the group of onlookers on the corner has grown.

They hide when the guerrillas fire, and peek out when they cease fire.

What's that all about?

When this round of firing stops, three boys appear, who run to collect the shell casings.

Same thing at the school: two boys gather up shells and seem to be hugely enjoying themselves.

13:00 A group of five comes to join the guerrillas on the corner: heavier weapons.

One with a ski mask.

They fire at the State Judicial Police.

You can hear the shattering of broken glass after the shots.

Heavy gunfire.

Another round begins.

They're all shooting.

Afterwards, they leave.

The previous group stays.

Again, the boys pounce on the casings.

And the onlookers.

Long silence.

13:25 Seems like they left.

People gather on the corner.

First, the boys who run collecting shells, then the grownups.

A blue Volkswagen arrives, and the driver talks to people.

Now everybody's running.

The armed men return.

Pass by, running toward the town creek.

From the Chacashib mountain range, in the west, innumerable waters spring.

Three creeks run through the town before merging with the Virgin River.

The one in the middle is the town's creek, and lies two blocks from the house.

There, we learned to swim.

In its crystal-clear waters my childhood was reflected.

In la Cidra pond.

In the pool of el Chorro, with its powerful waterfall.

In the multiple small pools where we used to catch crabs and small shrimp.

In that direction the men are running now.

13:28 A red truck passes by, toward the center of town.

Two more pass by.

"Eleuterio goes around transporting them," they say in the store.

13:29 Calm.

Vast Silence.

Roosters crow in the middle of the day.

There're no motors, nor radio, nor scandal.

You can hear everything, like in the *Good Old Days*.

"This is old Samuel's doing," my aunt says.

"It's a joke," says Luis.

"Many do-nothing bureaucrats as there are in Government and somehow the guerrillas managed to infiltrate everywhere, even in San Cristóbal," my father says.

Phone call from San Cristóbal: the Army is flying over the city.

The Army's already on its way here.

Same old song on the radio: "advancing toward the nation's capital conquering the Mexican Army."

And the rebel announcer enunciates each letter, defiant, proud.

The town is theirs.

There are flashes of brilliance and moments of naïveté in that speech.

I think about CCH East or about the touching "socialism" of the public preparatory schools that had some overexcited students shouting: "Give me free prep or give me death!"

I remember my surprise on arriving in my valley in recent years.

On entering the town and finding graffiti like "Proletarian Line Traitors" on one of the walls of Pancho Vásquez' house.

Or "Free dr. Felipe Sorano," in Temó, Chiapas.[11]

Or simply "Procup."

And those people?, I wondered, what are they doing so far from home?

And asking around and asking around, one gets drunk on a cocktail of acronyms: PROCUP[12]; PDLP[13]; GPP[14]; CIOAC[15]; OCEZ[16]; ACIEZ[17], ANCIEZ[18], UNORCA[19], ARIC[20], CNC[21], and ETC.

And everybody knows bits and pieces of the history.

There are even formal studies, some quite lengthy, about the political organizations working the jungle.

I remember one serious study about Las Cañadas that the ICHC[22], a state government institution, published some two or three years ago, it must be.

It talks about the work of the Liberation Theology catechists and their diligent labor to establish "the rein of God" in Lacandonia.

It talks about PROCUP and its party line of Prolonged Popular War.

It talks about the Poor People's Party.

The townspeople still remember the Engineer Cardel, who lived in Ocosingo for many years, and was detained by the FALN (Armed Forces of National Liberation), who used to have a training camp in El Diamante, Chiapas.

It's known that Maoist groups like Política Popular, the Proletarian Line, the Mass Line and the Leading Ideological Organization were there 20 years ago.

ARIC-UNION OF UNIONS and UNORCA derive from that era.

My wife explains to me that Política Popular split off into the Mass Line and the Proletarian Line, due to who knows what disagreements among the leadership, when they were working in the north.

"OID used to be part of the same group, though I don't remember what the fuss was about. The ones from Mass Line were organizing the government telephone company workers when Josie[23] and I got there to work with the women," my wife adds, remembering the Good Old Days.

"What're you writing, rabble-rouser?," she now asks, divining something in my smile.

Anyway, it's widely known that the political activists and the catechists were working together.[24]

"If they're not one and the same, they have something to do with it."

"Each goes his separate way, but hand in hand," my brother Rodulfo says.

13:41 Two men go quickly toward the creek; one with camouflage pants on, the other one in black.

13:43 The group from the school reappears.

Don Pablo, aunt Maga's husband, says they held up the Serfín bank in San Cristóbal.

13:54 A gunshot in the direction of the park.

14:00 Television news: *24 Horas.*
They completely downplay the extent of the problem.
Or don't know.
Nothing about the Declaration of War.

They talk about an armed indigenous group.
They're referring to San Cristóbal.
A telephone call comes in to give more accurate information, but about San Cristóbal.
They know nothing about what's going on here.

14:25 A man on a motorcycle passes by.
He's coming from the park.
Seems to get along well with the guerrillas, although he's wearing a T-shirt and short pants.

Passes calmly among the armed men from the school.

Stops his motorcycle and shouts: "Set that fucking thing on fire once and for all, buddy boy! There's the gasoline!"

And he laughs.

He's referring to a pick-up truck parked opposite the State Judicial Police building, right across the street, on Dora Cashcarita's sidewalk. The one on the bike comes up our street.

"That guy lives up here, and has been going around helping them since this morning," they say in the store.

"Well, isn't that Eleuterio's son?"

"They say his wife's a Salvadoran he brought home from the jungle."

"Oh, God, Ocosingo's full of Salvadorans... especially in this neighborhood up here, San Rafael."

14:40 Paca, another niece, comes running to the dining room.

"Uncle, now they set the truck on fire."

I go out quickly.

Flames underneath the truck.

Explosion: the tires.

The fire spreads.

Thick black smoke.

You can see people moving inside the house.

They go out the second-floor corridor.

They scream, panic-stricken: women and children.

Now you can see them through the corridor.

They're several of them.

You can see them stoop, suddenly appear, run, but inside the house.

They walk along a concrete wall.

Disappear.

Now they reappear and begin to take small children out along the concrete wall attached to cousin Toño's house.

Cries for help.

Some onlookers from the corner run to help.

Armed men, unmoved.

With the flames leaping so high, the house could burn
down.

If the car blows up, the house'll burn down.

The onlookers take the little children into their arms
across the concrete wall.

The women, men jump over.

More screams.

The last woman leaves.

They go up the sidewalk toward don Beto Ruiz's house,
here on the corner.

No effort to fight the fire.

Nothing can be done.

They're no firemen in town.

Besides, there's no water.

That was the biggest problem up until yesterday: a town
surrounded by water, criss-crossed by three creeks, has no
water because the municipal administration changed chiefs;
and the new chief, a civil engineer who "to make matters
worse isn't even from here," caused the valves to blow and the
hydraulic system to be ruined. Right in the middle of the New
Year's holidays.

The mayor "was in Tuxtla," or didn't show up for some
reason.

The throng of onlookers, above, has grown to about 100
people.

At the corner below, my uncle José Arcadio passes by,
shouting: "Let's do something! We're helpless! We can't just
be spectators!"

And we all wanted to do something.

But we don't know what.

We don't even have water to put out the car fire.

Nor the determination to pass among the armed men to
extinguish what they started and now, smiling, are watching
burn.

14:58 Pancho and Marco, Toño's sons, come to ask us to
keep their truck over here.

"In case the fire spreads."

Sure you can.

15:05 I open the gate.

I watch Toño take out his truck and come up here.

He enters.

We say hello to each other.

We chat.

Last night, after 1 o'clock in the morning, we went to wish them Happy New Year.

After dinner, either they come over here or we go over there.

Before, we used to have holiday dinner together: aunt Flor's family and my mother's family.

Now there're so many of us in each family that we no longer get together except to wish each other Happy New Year.

Last night we did it at about one o'clock.

The town was already being invaded.

We didn't realize.

15:15 Shattering glass thunders in the burning house.

15:22 More gunshots.

The flames from the pick-up truck die down.

Seems the house is saved now, despite the blackened walls.

Gunshots continue.

Toño tells me they took Chibeto and his whole family out of their house.

That they needed the house as an observation point.

That they didn't hurt them much.

They're at his sister-in-law Estela's house now.

More shooting.

More tear gas.

From the inner terrace, puffs of smoke are seen after the shots.

The guerrillas are firing at town hall, and from there they're responding with tear gas.

15:41 Movement in the upper stories of town hall.

Screaming and shouting.

White flags waving in peace.

Lots of white flags.

15:43 The screaming and shouting increases.

Public Safety surrendered!

People peek out.

Rumor, at the top of its lungs, scorches the street: "They surrendered already! They already gave up!

An immense roar is heard all over town.

"Now what?"

The vanquished policemen must be coming out and the rebels are cheering.

15:57 The guerrillas run down from the school protecting themselves in doorways and covering each other, military style.

Radio Villahermosa reports that 500 soldiers are coming from Palenque.

I go out the medical office door.

Lots of people look out at the corner, cautiously.

Venture out a bit more.

Now they come out, a yard or two, leaning forward, looking toward the park.

A compact little heap of onlookers.

A man arrives, from behind, stealthy.

Suddenly he shouts, "Boom!"

Everybody flinches.

First laughter in a long time.

More and more people pile up.

I go to the corner.

Rumors: that they dynamited the la Florida bridge (the one coming from San Cristóbal) and the Virgin River bridge (the one leading to Palenque).

I don't think so: we'd have heard it.

The latter is very close by.

That they burned down San Cristóbal city hall.

That they burned down the cattle-breeders' association buildings here.

But we can't see any smoke in that direction.

16:13 Three men on the corner.

Uniforms.

Little machetes.

Red bandanas.

Another group breaks open with their rifle butts the State Judicial Police door.

Those on the corner watch their backs.

Over there, next to the ones breaking open the door, a large group watching.

16:18 They open the offices and take a man with a white shirt on.

Take things, and search the room and small patio.

Apparently, the commandant was the last one left.

The other State Judicial Police had already escaped since morning.

A group of guerrillas takes the man in the white shirt toward the park.

16:21 A pelibuey sheep goes *b-a-a-a* amid the multitude looking out from the offices of the State Judicial Police or counting bullet holes on doors and walls.

The sheep continues, bleating, all the way to the corner.

A vivid image of forlorn abandonment.

That's how many of us are now: a lost flock.

16:37 The radio: "Attention, people of Mexico. At this time, *Radio Zapata* is reporting: as of this moment they inform us that Public Safety forces on this front have surrendered to EZLN forces."

16:58 Rumor on the corner: "They killed the State Judicial Police commandant."

"'Good afternoon,' he came out saying, with his hands in the air."

"Some broad let him have it, right here at the gates."

"That big black one, the one that looks like a man, a captain or who knows what, put a gun to his head and fired: everyone was shocked."

"Surrendered my foot! They put a hole in his head! He was lying right there, at the town hall gates."

17:03 Dora and Genner will be going down to the park.
Rodulfo and my wife will be going down, too.

17:05 Ovidio and Mario return.
More news: they have hostages at the cattle-breeders' association.
Don Enrique, Luis Pascasio, Dr. Talango, Rolando Pascasio and another of Don Enrique's sons-in-law.

17:33 My wife returns.
Shocked.
The dead in pools of blood.
Red handprints on the town hall columns.
They have 40 policemen tied up, with no shirts on, sitting on the floor.
"With their hands tied behind their backs."
"There they are, faces dumbstruck and full of fear."
"They're going to use them to negotiate Salinas' ouster."
I gaze upon the splendid afternoon.
The blue sky.
There are dense white clouds over the eastern hills, as if rent by an orange sun.
Call comes in from Tijuana: it's my mother-in-law.
Everybody in the States knows the news already.
Calls come in, but aren't going out.

17:44 "El Despertador Mexicano" ("The Mexican Wake Up Call") is the EZLN's organ of print communication.

On *Radio Zapata* they say that in their latest issue they're publishing the Declaration of War on the government and on the Federal Army.

There's no water in town.

Shadows begin to fall.
Clouds above the hills are growing denser.

17:52 A hymn on the radio: "Glory be to God./Glory be to the patron saint of our land, El Salvador./I shall be reunited with my people in the Cathedral/ to celebrate our great Patron Saint's day./And let there be life and liberty/in our land, El Salvador." That rings a bell.

18:00 Radio Zapata broadcasts a catchy ditty in octosyllabic verse accompanied by percussion.
Very talented for the most part, though the chorus is awful.
The rest is entertaining.
The verselets are broadcasting nothing less than a formula for making explosives!

18:10 My brother Rodulfo is going to go sleep at his house.
He and Conchita, his wife, have been here all day.
My mother doesn't want them to go, but Rodulfo insists.

I remember now that Mario said the insurgents dug trenches to render the runway useless, and that there were guerrillas positioned all along the landing strip to hinder any descent.
"The men are out there in the weeds, covered by the undergrowth."

It's cold.
Night has fallen.
They've turned the street lights on.

A group of six guerrillas have been on guard at the corner all afternoon.

On every corner there are similar security details.

18:46 News from San Cristóbal.

That there are five lookouts on every corner.

That cars with bullhorns are passing by, instructing people not to leave their houses.

On the radio they're saying they won't allow the EZLN to be discredited as a group of narco-traffickers, narco-guerrillas or bandits.

I feel tired.

I've eaten very little, but am not hungry.

Haven't stopped writing.

We wanted news, but the only thing on TV is *Don Francisco*, on one channel, and American football on the other.

"If only the Zapatistas could liberate us from this junk," I say to my wife.

"And what if they give us José de Molina instead?," she retorts and leaves me speechless.

Over the radio I hear, for the umpteenth time, that the insurgents' flag bears the colors red and black.

They call upon us to join the armed struggle.

Demand that Congress depose the "dictator."

Urge their troops to continue on in their campaign to advance upon the Mexican capital.

"Liberated" peoples shall be permitted freely to choose their own administrative authority.

The lives of prisoners shall be respected.

There shall be summary trials and members of the police and Army who've received foreign training or advisement shall be executed.

They stand accused, from this moment forward, of treason against the Homeland.

But those who submit to their authority shall be respected.

The enemy Army's surrender shall be demanded before every battle.

20:15 Chatter in the dining room.

Aunt Maga: The damned bishop has gone as far as to...

Me: I don't think he has anything to do with it: the church says it doesn't sanction bringing about change through force, that it rejects violence. If the bishop weren't here, the uprising would've happened long before.

Dora: Well, maybe you and the bishop will say mass, but...

20:20 My children call, from Mexico City.

We explain the situation to them and calm them down as much as possible.

I ask that they keep calling at this same time every day.

20:34 A gunshot.

21:15 A call from Mexico City, Josie.

She says that *Radio Mil* was reporting and interviewing people.

Talks about a conceited leader speaking English with tourists in San Cristóbal.

Confirms that this is a large-scale, joint operation, that she and Edgar have been monitoring the situation but can't see where it's coming from.

21:57 I've had a slight headache all day.

Since the first tear gas canister, I think.

22:22 Josie calls again.

Saying that Patrocinio González is already in Chiapas.[25]

That they interviewed guerrillas in San Cristóbal: they want the president and his entire cabinet to resign.

Channel 2 airs "the best of '93."

A little while ago, "Candid Camera."

While tension hangs over the town, national TV is broadcasting this garbage.

How isolated we feel.

What helplessness.

A phrase overheard this morning comes to me: we're so far from everything.

Or so we thought.

01:35 Images from San Cristóbal on the news.

Statements from the Federal and State governments.

They interview two guerrillas.

Everything seems different there: neither Central Americans, nor bossy people, nor violence, nor hostages, nor attacks on civilians, nor dead bodies.

And the guerrillas being interviewed are clearly indigenous.

Because of tourism and the San Cristóbal press?

Image control?

But *24 Hours* censors the Declaration of War.

They pass it all off as indigenous or peasant demands of minor importance.

The government offers dialogue.

Declare the Army will not intervene.

The images show access points to the city blocked by huge pine trees that have been cut down.

The news goes off.

A feeling of unease: everything seems so strange.

I lean out from the terrace overlooking the street, from the part under construction.

The rebels guarding the corner sleep, curled up in a ball, on the sidewalk.

I think I see one sitting on the doorstep of don Beto Ruiz' house.

I'm making this last entry at 2:39 a.m.

It's already another day.

My wife's waiting for me in the warm bed.

A thought occurs to me: reality is always right.

Come what may.

2 JANUARY[26]

8:15 Splendidly beautiful day: intense sun and blue sky.
Big cloud of smoke at town hall.

Nine guerrillas on the corner.

Indigenous Tzeltals all.

Nothing on the radio: "They smashed the station to pieces," Dora reports.

They turned the policemen loose: some of them passed this way, freezing to death, without shirts, without shoes, without socks.

Some of them in T-shirts.

"They were treating us like shit in there all night."

"Seems we saved our skins for now, but they say war is imminent."

Lots of rumors.

They opened up the ISSSTE store, and are going to burn it down.[27]

But first they're looting it.

They already burned the Office of the Superintendent of Preschool Education.

People pass through the streets with looted products.

A swarming anthill: from the corner, I see people with their cargo heading towards all four points of the compass.

Scores of people with boxes of "Patrona" cooking oil.

Children, teens, women and adult men pass by carrying merchandise.

There's a joyous gleam in their eyes.

Something like embarrassment in their posture.

Those who know each other don't look each other in the eye, or look at one another as if apologetically.

Or that's how I read it.

One person's carrying a cash register.

Another passes by, pushing, with a kitchen stove.

There's somebody bringing boxes on a dolly.

"Even people with money were stealing a while ago."

"One fat guy even brought a pick-up truck to carry off refrigerators."

I've returned to the house gate.

Three guerrillas have seen me taking notes, and come over here.

Stop in front of us.

Speak in Tzeltal.[28]

I stop taking notes.

§

Surely, taking notes isn't high treason?

I looked them in the eye, and said "Good morning."

Only one answered.

They left.

I feel my blood racing.

I want to smile to calm myself down but the truth is that it scares me.

This is helplessness.

The mass of poor people with their boxes never seems to end.

More rumors reach us: now they burned the six cars at Enrique Solórzano's house.

"Reduced to sheer metal."

9:37 The crowd of people has somewhat thinned out.

A boy passes by, saying: "It's all gone already."

One woman asks another, "Got some stuff, didn't cha," (mixture of affirmative and interrogative), which is responded to with, "Well, so what, if they're just gonna burn it all. They're givin' it away."

The news has spread all morning throughout the family's small universe: that the Army will come at 2 o'clock; that you're not supposed to say so, even though everybody seems to know it.

The news circulated by word of mouth and by telephone.

That Chelo, the tortilla lady, sent them a truckload of tortillas, and gave them coffee; that her husband is a PRD rep.[29]

That she didn't give it to them; they asked her.

That they also asked the driver to hand out the tortillas to the small group of guard patrols on each corner.

That she agreed to give all that away in exchange for their not ruining her business.

9:46 A call from San Cristóbal.

Saying the city was evacuated at one in the morning.

The EZLN left.

No one's there.

People are in the streets.

That a young man named Ortega was stopped at a Zapatista roadblock.

He stopped, but after talking, insisted on passing through by force.

They put a bullet in his head.

That traffic on the San Cristóbal-Comitán highway's cleared up now.

The problem, now, is Ocosingo.

10:00 Airplane noise.

We peek out and scope the sky.

Can't see anything.

Noise disappears.

10:09 We go shopping.

Dora and Génner, aunt Maga and don Pablo already went.

10:29 We return from shopping.

Brought back flour, corn meal, cooking oil and beans.

The store's called "La Costeña," and is making a killing.

An adolescent girl, chubby and red-faced, sweaty, can hardly keep up with all the customers.

The owner says he went with a group to pick up the policemen's dead bodies and put them in boxes.

"They killed the commandant there, at the town hall portico, and since they set fire to the prosecutor's office next, just as we were going to pick it up the body was already catching on fire. We asked those men's permission, and they refused, until we spoke with the priest; him they obeyed. That's how we picked up the dead. This already half scorched kid."

On the corner, among the people, agitated, we meet up with Gabriel and Isaías.

They're sons of Mariano, who was in charge of our ranch for many years.

My father sold him 12 acres, and there they live now.

Isaías still works with my father: he drives the pick-up truck and helps with the coffee grinding and drying.

Gabriel now works as a driver for Conasupo, in Oxchuc.

They look worried.

Isaías says that all night long the guerrillas passed through the ranch: "They come and go, come and go."

They pass through to ask for water, don't talk, don't say anything.

They only ask for water.

"They're nothing but second valley 'settlers.'"

(The ranch lies to the southeast of town, ten minutes from the Virgin River, toward Toniná,[30] in the area of ranches that stretches all the way to the second valley.

Arriving at the ranch of don Ángel Cañas—now deceased: the ranch now belongs to Aladino, his son-in-law, and to Hada, his daughter—you have to follow the clearing on the left; just up ahead lies Coelhá, our family property: 198 acres of cattle and coffee plantations. Plus a hill my father re-forested, and which is the only patch of intense green amid the hills of nearby ranches, all converted to pasture now.

My parents preserve the coffee plantations and the woodland that shades the coffee trees, even though the price of coffee is low.

They'll never allow the old forest to become pasture. Even though livestock is a safe business and the price of coffee keeps falling.

There're people who've already chopped down their coffee plantations.

But the forest is sacred, coffee too.)

Smells like smoke.
They set fire to town hall.

10:34 The armed men from the corner went toward the park.

Everybody went down.

I go to the corner, hear the following dialogue:

—And the guys from Public Safety, where were they?

—Holed up there in town hall.

—And why weren't they shooting, then?

—Because they didn't have orders from the governor.

—Oh, that's bullshit; well, then what'd they come for?

We go down to the park.

Stop in at the offices of the judicial state police.

Doors and walls reveal hundreds of bullet marks.

Dora and Carlos Cisneros' house reveals the abundance of smoke that the burning pick-up truck left on it.

The flames almost got inside.

There're no longer any rebels here, nor at the school, nor on the next block over.

We arrive at the park.

Spray paint on the municipal building wall overlooking Avenida Central: "We be back soon."

More graffiti on the portico: "Long live the insurgents."

Blood on the pillars.

I go through the corridor to the extreme left.

In the first office on the left, desks, file cabinets, chairs are burning.

The bonfire is almost consumed.

You can see a water tank amid the twisted metal.

It used to be the prosecutor's office.

Ash, smoke, glowing embers, blasts of oven heat.

Second office from left to right: fire still burning from desks, huge pile of ash, lamps on the floor.

Remnants of jackets, blankets, rolls of wire, chairs, car license plates, stationery.

Second floor lobby: burning.

Papers, balls, shoes, typewriters, bicycles: all amidst the smoky ash and heat.

Desk supplies, chairs, storage batteries, remains of a very old photo of the park.

People gawk, whisper.

I go back a few steps, to the prosecutor's office once again.

I see the half-dried pool of blood and the line it traces.

I measure it: twelve long paces, dried blood, on the park floor tile.

A comment: "It's the commandant's. He came out with his hands up but they put a bullet in him anyway."

Bloody footprints, from bloody shoes.

More graffiti: "Z.A. Zapatista Army."

I return through the corridor: oven vapors come out from each door.

Blackened ceiling of the corridors.

The third office, from left to right, like the ones before, is burning.

Here just ashes and briefly glowing embers.

But the last office is intact: the doors closed and untouched.

Only reveals a large-caliber bullet hole in a small announcement display window.

"Here they didn't do anything because it's the treasury office: the names of people and their properties are here. This way, they can collect the war tax."

I go down to the park: on the ground a jacket, a T-shirt, tin cans, a crate of soft drinks.

A Public Safety squad car, shot up, in the middle of the street.

Some socks.

On the second floor of town hall everything seems to have been burned: it's steaming hot.

The glass, first broken by gunfire, ended up being blown out by the fire.

Here, in front of the municipal building, in the center, a pile of equipment: three typewriters, a motor, a machine where they make voter registration cards.

Some pants from the Public Safety uniform and a backpack.

There're crates of soft drinks scattered about the park, sardine cans, boxes of cookies, tetrapak juice containers.

Another Public Safety truck, blue, with the windows shot out.

And shoes, boots, police uniform jackets.

A man, one of the town's crazy people, gathers up some shoes, sits on a park bench, takes off his own and puts on the ones he just collected.

Many look at him and laugh.

He seems not to notice.

Finishes.

Leaves.

Church bells toll infinitely gently now.

The small church bell rings tenderly, thinning out the mid-morning air.

I find myself thinking about the bell ringer from *Al filo del agua*.31

55-gallon barrels, tires, people in front of the church.

"There's going to be a Mass for the Dead."

People pile up at the entrance.

We go over.

There's a truck with caskets. They arrange them.

There's a priest up above.

We're about 20 paces away when the truck sets off toward the cemetery.

"There wasn't any Mass," people say.

To the left of the church and convent, with its beautiful colonial roof tiles, just across the street, there's a corner house.

It was donated to the municipality.

It could have been be a charming museum or a lovely house of culture, right in the middle of downtown, and with all the features of the elegant old construction.

The mayors' ignorance has stuck everything in there: they've used it as a PRI headquarters and now as judicial offices: Joint Federal District Trial Court.[32]

Lots of smoke.

Heaps of files are still burning.

I calculate some 20 cubic feet of ash.

Everything burned.

As if to wipe out every trace, all memory.

As if to start all over again.

People walk around the street looking, keeping an eye out, asking, wondering.

Suddenly, everybody runs.

The crazed multitude.

I take my wife by the hand.

We run toward the house.

Straight ahead.

I see my cousin and my sister.

Anguished faces.

"Let's go," we shout to each other, and flee amid the multitude.

Passing the park we halt our step.

What happened?

Nobody knows exactly, but it's all becoming clear.

The guerrillas grouped up at the marketplace.

Someone came to warn them there was a skirmish at La Cumbre, a rural restaurant on the way to Palenque, before you get to Jotolá, where they made the detour to get to the oil well whose steel tower is an eyesore on the horizon.

It lies in the blue ridge mountains, to the northwest.

"What happened was the Federal Army was coming and the guerrillas who were about to take Palenque ambushed them at La Cumbre."

"They came to warn them about that, or warned them by radio."

"We don't know who won."

"That's why the agitation started, and suddenly everybody started running like mad when the guerrillas started gathering."

We just passed the Banamex buildings.[33]

Windows shot out.

"They took the money."

Surely, it can't be so easy to open a safe?

"They blew the bank vault."

How?

"With dynamite."

But we didn't hear that either, and we're two and a half blocks away.

On the inside you can see disorder, but disorder of minor proportions: papers strewn about, articles rummaged through, but no trace of an explosion.

"They made off with the bills and tossed the loose change out among the people."

"You saw them?"

"No, people told me."

The guerrillas haven't gone: they're at the marketplace.

About half left already, but three or four hundred remain.

They're going to open the big businesses over there.

10:57 Sound of a plane or helicopter.

Can't see it.

Yep, there it is.

Flies over the airfield, over by the park.

Descends, but not too much.

Has some letters that can't be seen with the naked eye.

With the binoculars we read CHIAPAS on the green and white helicopter.

Before my very eyes, a yard away, a blue dragonfly passes by.

"Now we're talkin': there was nothing left from the ISSSTE store but now they're opening La Suriana," announces a child herald running by.

A while ago we saw a barefoot Tzeltal going down the street.

The man, as if ill, was taking small steps forward.

Was going to the ISSSTE store.

Some people told him to hurry because the divvying up was almost over already.

The man continued with his slow baby steps.

Now I see him on the way back, up the way, barely walking with his barefoot little steps, clutching his part of the booty to his chest: a box of Kotex.

He doesn't know what he's carrying, but that was his share.

And the looting continues: a man comes carrying a swivel chair.

Another carries off two regular chairs.

One boy can barely manage a huge roll of yellow cloth.

Someone goes off with a radio.

"There were even VCRs."

"El Pedro ripped off a TV."

A boy goes by with a shiny little battle tank, made out of blue plastic: "It's gonna be my little brother's Twelfth Night gift," he says. [34]

A young man with a typewriter.

Yesterday's drunken bricklayers have passed by several times carrying boxes.

Now one of them passes by pushing a green hand truck with tree boxes: two of Bacardi rum and one of Presidente brandy.

The Jaguar will get a rest.

A woman says: "Rich people shouldn't touch anything. Us, we're poor, so..."

"Doggone thieves," my sister Dora whispers.

Surely, she's fearing for her own store "Novedades Teté," next to whose door we're standing.

A boy passes by with clothing: denim jackets and shirts: a good-sized bundle, about 20.

Tittle-tattle in Carmelino's store.

The customers talk, grouped on the sidewalk.

I listen and record:

"Ms. Yaya Solórzano went to take don Enrique his pill, and when she saw how they had him all tied up, she sees him and, my oh my, she faints clean away!"

"Miss Toni Trejo wanted to give don Enrique his medicine, too, but they didn't give her permission. They're holding them there: don Enrique and his sons-in-law; and Luis Pascasio and his son."

"They say they kidnapped don Enrique up because his father, don José, used to flog his workers on El Rosario and in the montería."

"Don José didn't hardly have no montería."

"Well, he most certainly did; I believe he had a chiclería, too."[35]

"But don José, he died back way back when. These Injuns hadn't even been born."

(And the name Pedro de Solórzano comes to mind, 16th century encomendero,[36] commissioned by the then governor of these lands, the adelantado don Francisco de Montejo, to pacify the Godless and rebellious Indians, who kept the Spanish advance through these fertile valleys in constant peril.

Pedro de Solórzano was never able to pacify the region: only to hold the indigenous peoples in check.

From here to Tenosique, the jungle was Chol and Tzeltal territory for the remainder of the 16th Century, and so remained for 300 years more, in a state of permanent war.

"Sole libertarian bastion within New Spain," some say.

The Ladino dominion in the second valley began in the second half of the 19th century, with the first explorers.

Don Juan Ballinas charted the course of the Jataté River and dreamed of a road that might reach Tabasco and enable commerce and communication.

Those who took advantage of don Juan's efforts were the "woodsmen": exploiters precious woods that were logged via the Usumacinta River.

Traven has written about them in *The Rebellion of the Hanged*.[37]

And also Pablo Montañez (don Pedro Vega), in *Lacandonia* *(1961)*, *Jataté-Usumacinta (1971)*, and *La agonía de la selva (1973)*.[38]

Traven: the outsider's vision.

Montañez: the insider's vision.

Granted the differences between the great writer and the amateur, Montañez' almost autobiographical novels are illustrative and moving.

Well, then, that was don Pedro de Solórzano, the first in this valley where there are now so many Solórzanos, rich and poor.

The "infidels" remained in libertarian turmoil for more than 300 years.

Then they thinned out or were displaced to the north of the state.

"The Indians from there eat people," was the old wives' tale up until the era of don Juan Ballinas.

There were many incursions upon Ocosingo.

Now they've returned.

The jungle has memory.)

But the looting continues: a man passes by with blankets: six.

There's a small knot of women on the corner.

—And you Julia... what'd ya make off with?

—Whole buncha cunt rags.

—Oh, yeah?

—Yep, pure Kotex. But like this, see—and she makes a gesture with her arms indicating a pile about two feet high—so, sue me! It's just that, poor pussy, she works so hard... Gotta treat her right: I already gave her a pack.[39]

And the woman bursts into shrill laughter, showing her gold teeth.

Everybody in the little group cracks up laughing.

11:15 The looting of La Suriana continues.

People pass by carrying bales of clothing, big bales.

And towels, pants, blankets, shirts, T-shirts.

Everyone's invited: "Hurry up. Everybody's grabbing stuff."

And other women, under their breath, in a low voice, and right out loud, crack their disapproving whips: "Why, they have no shame," "Thieving bitches," "Why, it doesn't bother them to go and steal," "It's because they're from Oxchuc," "It's because they're not from around here," "Why not, even people from here are stealing now; lots of people are going around carrying their bundle; if only you'd seen them down there: a swarming anthill of thieves."

"Even Doctor Segundo was in the ISSSTE store," "Even people from Morales photo shop," "The Cocheco family even carried off big appliances by car," "Like the big fat guy from Superior brewing distributor," "Even Ms. Carmen from up the way," "Ms. Odila carried off a television," "la Trini," "El Ramón, la Tosferina's son."

A young man passes by with a sackful of Nido brand milk containers.

A lady asks him if he'll sell her a can.

He responds: "You're kiddin' me, right, teach?"

"No, seriously, it's for my little kids. I didn't get to buy any."

"Yeah, right... gimme a break."

We go back to the park.

There're people and solitude in a strange silence.

They say the rich are sheltered in humble houses: with their ranch hands or their maids.

We cross the park and the plaza amid the thrown out clothes and boxes, and tin cans, and jars and shoes.

We cross the plaza, headed toward the church.

12:42 We enter the great empty church. Natural light passes through the magnificent arches of the church windows. Illuminates enormous walls of white stone.

I contemplate the imposing beam work of the ceiling and the visible roof tiles.

I look at the altars: the niches and the walls decorated with river pebbles of varying colors.

The Nativity occupying the altar front.

(After the "burning of the saints," during the period of don Victórico Grajales, the church remained empty. My great-grandmother, doña Angélica Ballinas, donated two wooden sculptures, life-sized, by the Guatemalan sculptor Julio Dubois. The Christ Child, also made of wood and life-sized, by the same sculptor, my mother keeps.)

There's no one in the enormous nave.

We pause to contemplate the great cedar portal and its door latches.

It's still unvarnished, and smells delightful.

El Beto Gutiérrez made it, bricklayer, carpenter, electrician, witch doctor, sorcerer.

He dreamed, he told me a few days ago, that "there was a lot of hanging meat... it was like a huge space... but the meat was beginning to rot... was already stinking. I woke up sweating. Maybe something's going to happen."

Here's how recounts his dreams.

He squints his already tiny eyes and speaks slowly, as if looking far away.

We go out into the street.

People descend rapidly upon the looting of La Suriana, which continues.

Another helicopter.

"There're about 300 guerrillas in the marketplace. They've got don Enrique and the others there. They also have other men tied up, Indians from around here. Who knows why."

We take the road down from the church, toward the cemetery.

Reach Jorge Ordóñez' house.

Take a right turn to go back home.

Meet up with Alfonso Cruz, a friend.

Hugs, joy, conversation.

He's the son of don José Cruz, brother of Armando, owners of Toniná, the ranch on whose land is located the archeological site where my wife has worked at the end of the last four digging seasons.

Alfonso came from the ranch on horseback because his daughters are here with their grandparents.

"I came to look in on them because gunshots were heard and I was worried. Socorro didn't let me come, but it's better to see that they're safe."

This afternoon he'll return to the ranch with Antonino, his cousin and, like him, conservator of the archeological site.

We make plans to go to Toniná on Friday and eat there.

Carlos Espinoza, Alfonso's brother-in-law, chats with us.

Two more people, who aren't from town but work here, join in on the chat.

One of them reports: "Yesterday there were about 200 of them here in the street. This was all green. We encouraged each other and went out to talk here at the corner door. One of the Central Americans would talk, then answer his radio or shoot a burst of machine-gun fire into the air with a huge weapon. And if only you'd seen it, all the little Indians from around here, 'cause they brought several squads of Indians with imitation wooden rifles or little .22 rifles, they had them back here, in formation. When he would let loose with the burst of machine-gun fire, they would just cringe with their eyes closed and were shaking like a leaf. Poor bastards, it scared them."

13:01 I see little old man Martín coming with a roll of cloth wrapped in a plastic bag.

He lives on one of my father's properties.

Surely he saw us.

I pretend not to have seen him: continue with the conversation.

My wife does the same.

He passes right next to us with his gaze directed at the opposite wall, covering his face with the enormous roll, which he switched from one shoulder to the other.

Weird codes, these: we don't look at him so he won't feel ashamed, and he pretends not to have seen us.

Old Martín.

Alfonso interrogates some women: "And that, you... how much did it cost you?"

They don't answer him.

He harps on it with other people: "You, where're they selling stuff so cheap?

"Everybody's coming away with so much stuff. The sale must be good."

"You, where'd you buy that?"

"Yes, indeedy, free trade has now begun!"

13:10 They say there's fighting in Temó, or thereabouts.

A woman dressed in black passes by the corner below.

She's coming from church, headed toward the cemetery.

We head down a ways.

There she goes, through the half-deserted street.

"Looks like one of the policemen's widows," says a man with a hat on.

There she goes, alone, young, screeching in grief, along the empty street.

We say goodbye to Alfonso and company.

We go up to the house.

On the street they ask us if we're reporters: me, I haven't stopped writing and my wife is carrying her camera.

We meet up with Toño in front of aunt Flor's house.

Two indigenous types, dressed in civilian clothing, with black hats and radio equipment, have followed us all the way to the corner.

Since when?

Goosebumps.

I hadn't noticed them.

Toño pointed them out to us: someone had told him, a while back, that they were following us.

Those black hats look Guatemalan.

Guatemalan boogeymen?

My nieces, cousins go out.

We chat for a little while.

My cousin Eglantine says that today a man came out of her house, which adjoins the judicial state police.

Fearfully, he asked permission to flee from there, telling aunt Flor not to be afraid.

They don't know if he was a policeman or detainee.

He was hiding there when the guerrillas came in.

They didn't find him.

We talk about the fighting at La Cumbre.

That it did indeed take place but that the federal Army won and that now they're coming this way.

Someone reported it by phone or radio.

We continue home.

Pause with another group on the corner.

The one with the radio and the black hat plays dumb, sitting on Arístides' corner.

Someone reports: "The commandant was like this, with his head turned around this way. Just at that moment a female guerrilla captain passed by, a big black broad, curly-haired, the one who killed him, and using her big boot straightened out his head with a swift kick."

14:12 They say there's skirmishing in Rancho Nuevo.

A chemist, my brother Edgar's friend, just called.

He's from Villa las Rosas.

His family was going to San Cristóbal.

Came back from Mitzitón because there was fighting up ahead and it wasn't possible to get to San Cristóbal.

Another call: they looted the San Cristóbal IMSS store.

15:13 Another rumor scorching the street: that the Army already arrived.

That now they're coming over by the High School, at the town's entrance.

Screams.

Running.

A man comes by the school carrying a big piece of furniture.

I hear Carmelino shouting, "Eric! Eric! And la Enia... ?"

And so on: "Hurry up! They're coming now! Get inside! What the fuck you gonna look for down there?!"

Eric's now married and lives two houses up.

Has a store on the highway.

The furniture man stops at the school.

Peeks around the corner.

Hesitates.

Makes up his mind, finally, and crosses the street with his enormous cargo.

He comes up the street.

Rumor continues.

People walk home quickly.

Three men pass by and report: "There they come now, two blocks away. They're coming little by little, so as not to make noise."

And another: "Ah, so supposedly they've come all the way from Mexico City, that's why they never arrived."

"First they stopped to pray at la Villa; they came on their knees."[40]

"But... well, where are they, the sons of bitches?"

The rumor must have spread through the whole town already.

The man with the giant load reached Lety's corner.

"There they come now! There come the soldiers!"

The man crosses the corner, is approaching us.

Now we can identify what he's been carrying with such great effort: an enormous cedar countertop.

And the residual furniture and fixtures of looted stores parades before our eyes, amid the haste and alarming rumor.

A few minutes ago a man with a blender passed by.

We saw someone with a fan.

One with a mirror frame and another with the mirror.

In the last hour the number of people who were carrying shoes, rubber boots, sandals of various colors, increased.

"It's because they opened Calzamoda and there's a shitload of shoes."

"Even ceiling panels from the ISSSTE store were stolen."

"Right down to the light bulbs!"

Elías, Lety's husband, signals to us from the corner and yells out to us that now they're coming.

The ones on the other corner tipped him off.

Can it be?

The marketplace guerrillas were supposed to have left already.

"No," says Génner, "they were going to await the soldiers there."

"They say there're a lot of them hidden in houses and around town. As soon as the soldiers are in place they'll be hemmed in, and they're going finish them off. That's what some people from the marketplace were saying."

Shouts suddenly, as if muffled, as if subdued.

At the corner of the highway the first Army truck appears, at a very low speed.

The soldiers signal. "Get inside! Get inside!"

We're all looking out the doors and windows.

Another truck with soldiers and military gear.

And another, and yet another.

Some white buses follow, full of soldiers with arms at the ready.

Ten or twelve vehicles in total, counting the buses.

"Look over there!"

We see soldiers passing on foot through the school's street, advancing from north to south.

"Get inside! Get inside!," they signal urgently to all onlookers and to the few people still going about the street.

First shots below: three, like a signal, small caliber.

Now we go inside for sure, like everybody on our street.

Close the doors.

Go up to the second floor.

The last troop truck passed by, headed for the highway.

The countertop man, who'd remained frozen next to Eric's house, ten yards from his cargo, retrieves it now.

Last try.

Crosses the highway.

Disappears.

Whew!

From the terrace we see Toño on the roof of aunt Flor's house.

With his children.

Aura and I are here, on the terrace overlooking the street.

We scan the horizon trying to see where the soldiers will come down from, but you can't see anything.

Only sun on the silent streets that we do manage to see.

Let's hope the rebels have gone.

They've had all the time in the world, ever since the three warning shots were fired.

Surely, they were Zapatista lookouts alerting their comrades down below.

But nothing's happened.

"They're going to go down by Fitín's house," Aura says.

(The town ended there ten years ago: a street that didn't used to exist and which now leads down to the marketplace and the airfield.)

But the minutes pass and we don't see anything along that street.

"They took so long. I'm sure they went all the way to the Beltway."

(Yet more recent road work: it encircles the town from the gas station, on the highway from San Cristóbal, passes behind the cemetery and between the marketplace and the landing strip. It continues along La Parcela and joins the highway that goes to Yajalón.)

"That's great: it's a very good time for the guerrillas to have escaped."

"God willing."

15:45 The full afternoon sun returns the church to its magnificence.

Scant gray clouds.

Blue sky.

Intense greenery.

Remoteness.

15:50 "Let's hope they've gone." I think, while contemplating the fleeting transparency and silence.

15:52 The shoot-out thunders with unanticipated violence!

Heavy weapons.

Cross-fire.

A bit of smoke, which disappears immediately.

A deafening bang: like exaggerated cannon fire.

Intense exchange of gunfire.

Clacking of machine guns and fainter strafing, as if from submachine guns.

Violent rattling at full blast.

15:53 Cross-fire continues.

Thuds are heard as if from a bazooka or an enormous cannon.

Thuds are heard like bombs, although there're no helicopters or planes.

Another tremendous and hair-raising explosion.

What sounds like that?

What can it be?

I look out from the inner terrace, fearing the town will have been blown up or that the houses below will be in flames.

I poke my head out through the terrace's protective railing but everything's the same, everything's in its place.

No flames or smoke are seen.

Nothing's missing, apparently.

Air's clean.

And the deafening shoot-out, uninterrupted, tremendous.

Another thunderous impact.

Another loud bang like a bomb.

Another and yet another.

Like cannon fire.

"Must be bazookas," cousin Pablo says.

Machine-gun fire follows, the battle's joined.

Shelling.

Children and adults run through the house seeking refuge.

15:55 The intense cross-fire continues.

You can hear it behind the church, from north to south, in the direction of the marketplace and Port Arturo, over by the air field.

The Army didn't arrive by air.

15:57 Why didn't the guerrillas leave?

More cannon fire!

Minimal silence, broken by sub-machine guns and machine guns.

Heavy fire.

Continues.

More, more, more.

All from the same direction, in the eastern part of town, behind the church, from north to south.

Or, more precisely, from northeast to southeast.

15:59 Terrifying impact.

The whole town shakes and sways.

It shocks, impacts, batters the psyche, a bang of that magnitude.

I try not to stop writing.

I think the projectiles can't reach here but I write sitting on the ground, protected by the window wall and, a yard farther away, by the terrace wall.

I think about my mother and her heart.

Go downstairs.

For the first time I see her truly frightened and breathing with difficulty.

We take her to her room: she was with my father, in the living room, listening to the violent bangs, when the last horrific explosion rang out.

We're all protected on one side or another.

One thinks of a bomb blast capable of destroying town, of causing irreparable damage.

That's how the explosions sound.

I want to see.

I peer out very cautiously from the terrace overlooking the street; see two Army pick-up trucks pass by the school.

Another major impact!

But no sign in the direction it rang out from: neither smoke, nor flames, nor dust.

One thinks of bombs dropped from the air but there're no helicopter or airplane noises.

How I regret my military ignorance.

What can produce that altogether thunderous sound?

A grenade-launcher, a cannon, a bazooka?

And the medium-impact bangs?

16:02 Exchange of gunfire continues.
Another loud bang I can only think to call a "blast"!

16:03 As if something ripped through the air.
The bang makes one's blood boil.

I see the immovable church tower, and hear the tremendous silence after the stunning, paralyzing reverberation.

I think about Karen, Teté, Oswaldo, Ámbar, Paca, Arturo and Angélica, children between four and twelve years old, whom I saw a little while ago, face down, beneath the kitchen table.

Very serious: as if they were all eyes.

My nieces and nephews.

In the deep silence the cries of geese, blackbirds and roosters.

Afternoon aches in its infinite beauty.

I hear the clamor.

"War is imminent," policemen were saying this morning.
It's already here.
Flocks of blackbirds pass over the church.
Some lone herons.
A flock of pigeons flies above us.
Another perturbing explosion.

16:07 No one will believe the intense roar of the
detonations.
We want to record it, but the recorder doesn't turn up, or
it needs batteries, or there're no cassettes.

16:10 Shadows run on the second floor of town hall.
I focus the binoculars: soldiers.

16:12 The shoot-out continues in all its intensity.
Will this never end?
It's already lasted about 20 minutes.

16:17 An Army armored personnel vehicle comes down our
street.

16:20 The gunfire continues.
Total silence, for a few seconds, broken by this raging
gunfight.
A strange sound: like a terrifying screech piercing the air.
Paralyzes.
Like the sound of a jet plane racing at ground level.
Doesn't thunder.
Disappears.
What was that?

16:31 The firing hasn't ceased.
My mother is calm inside her room.
My nieces and sisters and brothers-in-law are also there.
"Here I am like a hen with her chicks," she says when I
appear.
"Don't be poking your head out, son. Be careful."

16:33 Another spectacular detonation.
Drumfire, intense.

16:38 Sub-machine gun at about 150 yards.
Then, silence.

The proximity is all the more chilling, though the burst of sub-machine gun fire seems almost toy-like, compared with the clamor below.

In the silence: the streaming of the water tank.

16:42 Gunfire and silence intermingling.
I'm writing on the second floor.

My wife brings up a tray of food: I put it on the windowsill I'm leaning against.

A delicious, steaming hot plate of chicken and rice.
Habanero sauce with lemon and a little red onion.
I'm seated on a bedroll, on the white marble floor.
I eat and write.
Life.

I think, now, that I set myself to write as a way of conquering defenselessness.

We all, in the house, do something to conquer it.

16:57 Another loud bang.
Isolated shots.

16:58 A huge racket.
Abundant submachine-gun fire.
The cross-fire, merciless, continues.
More shooting.
The echo reverberates in the high mountain range.
Heavy weapons.
Cannons, bazookas, grenade launchers?
How to know?
Just the loud bang and the long echo interrupted by ever more submachine-gun fire.
Silence.

I lean out, once more, over the street-side terrace, behind the part under construction.

Shots are heard very close by.

Elías and his son are at the door, on the corner.

They signal me to get inside, certainly because I'm high up.

I hide myself a bit.

Silence.

I count the seconds: 57.

There hasn't been a single minute without gunfire.

17:00 Three violent reports.

Yet another.

I gaze at palm trees, bougainvillea, lime trees, citron plants, grapefruit trees, orange trees, and tangerine trees in the town foliage.

A rooster crows at length.

Another bang.

Isolated shots of lesser audible impact.

Clouds in the distance, above blue hills.

The fighting of men below.

17:01 Silence.

17:05 More shelling. Then nothing.

17:07 Three isolated shots.

Birdsong.

17:09 Other isolated shots from small-caliber arms.

The firing seems to have ceased.

17:11 More gun and heavy weapons fire!

More heavy weapons slicing through the air!

Swallows begin to flutter amidst the loud bang.

Submachine-gun fire nearby.

17:15 Three loud bangs from heavy weapons.
Silence.

17:17 Still nothing.
Gunfire's become sporadic.
No: another short burst of machine-gun fire rings out.

17:20 Another tremendous reverberation!

17:23 Isolated shots.
Suddenly I'm paralyzed.
Goosebumps: a sound nearby on the tin roof of Arístides'
billiard hall.
Right there, across the lower patio.
Fright in the face of the muffled noise.
I look out and you can't see anything.
Suddenly it occurs to me it could have been a citron fruit.
Yes: a big citron fruit fell off the branch onto the tin roof.
Gulp!

17:26 Another tremendous explosion!

17:28 And yet another.
In the midst, silence nibbled away at by geese.

17:29 Another thud, to which a rooster's long, drawn out
crow seems to respond.

17:30 Once again the awful thunder.
The shadow entered the first valley.
The sun now beats down upon blue hills and above clouds
that cap the hilltops.
The blue mountain range becomes a blur to the right,
toward the beginning of the second valley, just past the hill of
El Paraíso, the estate don Juan Ballinas founded last century.
(When don Juan died, El Paraíso was inherited by his
children: uncle Cuauhtémoc and my great-grandmother,
Mamma Angelica. She ceded her lands from Agua Dulce to

our uncle, and came to live in town after the revolution.[41] In Agua Dulce my mother was born. Aunt Consuelo inherited El Paraíso from her father, uncle Guatimoc, and she, facing land-reform persecution on her homestead, Dolores, and on her inherited property, El Paraíso, began to sell it off.

It was painful, because the family history is safeguarded in the big house at El Paraíso. El Paraíso does honor to its name. In the beautiful foothills lies the orchard don Juan planted and uncle Cuauhtémoc made grow: cedar trees, sapodilla trees, sapote trees, mamey trees, cacao trees and coffee trees make up a dense cultivated foliage.

In whose midst rises a source of purest spring water. The stream runs between the vegetation, crosses a field of giant bamboo stalks—they form basins with the base of these yellow stems furrowed by green streaks—and surfaces at the house. A fork in the stream services the kitchen: running water from the clear spring, a sudden torrent, passes near the oven and the burners. Then it follows its course through the valley. Flows into more streams and thence to the Jataté River, the father river which is born near El Corralito and cleaves a path through the first valley. And this second valley. And shall so continue gathering ever greater waters, till such time as it joins with the Lacantun River and flows into the Usumacinta river system. So, this is the El Paraíso I remember. So I saw it as a child, when we would arrive there after a 12- to 14-hour day on horseback. It used to be said that aunt Consuelo suffered persecution from the advocates of land reform, who expropriated her land and sold it off. The last thing she preserved from El Paraíso was the big house, the orchard, the cemetery: 35 acres in all. My aunt Maga bought them when she left the big city. There are so many people in these valleys now. When don Juan came to lay the foundation for his house, in the mid 19th century, this was the great Desert of the Lacandon People, the Desert of Solitude. Since the Spanish incursions of the 16th and 17th centuries, few attempts had been made to traverse the jungle. Don Juan, with his scant resources wrested from the land, carried out reconnaissance expeditions of the Jataté River, to the extent he managed to traverse it. Reached, after several attempts spread out over the years, as far as Flores el Petén, in Guatemala. Named various rivers, lagoons, valleys and mountains. Produced the first map of the area. Wrote a memoir: *The Desert of the Lacandon People*, whose manuscript Frans Blom[42] and Gertrude Duby[43] discovered during one of their respites in El Paraíso, before entering the jungle. They promoted its publication, on behalf of the state government, in 1951. Three or four years ago, Rodrigo Núñez reissued it in Tuxtla Gutiérrez. And so it was. The great desert. *The solitary valleys, sylvan.*[44] But beginning in 1960 people came from all around. The government got out of a jam by parceling out lands in the jungle: people from Veracruz, from Michoacán, from Hidalgo, from Guerrero, arrived in these valleys. And came down from the highlands of Chiapas, and came from the north of the state. And the jungle decreased and the population increased. And the colonies grew and the communities, and the fire[45] and the cornfields and the pastures. And the basic necessities. And the noble redeemers who shall carry us off to paradise at gunpoint. Another paradise: that for which they kill each other here below.)

17:50 I lost my train of thought.
The din has continued and the gunshots.
And the violent thuds.
And the cry of geese intermingling with cross-fire.
Snatches of silence.
You can see some smoke near Port Arturo.
The beauty of late afternoon goes on increasing.
I change my observation point.
Look west.
Sun sets behind the Chacashib mountain range.
Beams of light beam forth as in ancient engravings.
When I saw those engravings in the Bible, for the first time, at the age of 11 or so, I "recognized" this image I see again now, amidst silence and gunfire.
I think of Díaz Mirón's[46] verse:
West-setting sun crowns august pinnacle

Just when it seems calm was restored, the firefight worsens.
Another startling roar!
When's this going to stop?

The light beams' beauty intensifies as they diminish.
The cannonade continues.
What's this?
Where're so many bullets coming from?
Did they really have the power to declare war?
So much resistance is inexplicable.
Yesterday, Alfonso Cruz's acquaintances were saying, the
rebels were showing off their armaments.
"We even got missiles," they said smiling.
But they must have something to put up so much
resistance.
A white car passes the corner at full speed.
The shoot-out rebegins below.

The shelling returns.
Intense, though less so than a while back.
There was a drunk on the corner.
Looked like Eulogio Trujillo.
I hear a nearby burst of heavy-weapon machine-gun fire.
Look out from behind the wall under construction.
You could hear it at the corner, but there's nobody there.
Eulogio, either, if that's who it was.

17:52 There's no longer light in the hills but the shoot-out
continues.

17:53 I see Carmelino on his balcony, barely leaning over.
They called him by phone from down below.
Saying there're lots of rebels holed up in the empty houses
of people who're on vacation.
That the bulk of the rebels are putting up resistance in the
marketplace and near the library.
That they've been occupying lone houses since last night.

But we've also heard gunshots, though fewer, along the river and over by the highway.

17:56 Another brutal explosion followed by a furious exchange of gunfire.

18:01 Intense heavy-weapons fire.

I go down to the dining room and meet nieces, nephews, brothers-in-law, brothers and uncles on the stairs, taking advantage of the double wall of protection.

The living room's big picture windows, which we so enjoy on normal days, now give us a sense of fragility.

Even though beyond the patio lies the concrete wall and then Arístides' house.

"But a grenade on the patio would finish us all off," says Rosario with her voice lowered.

Everybody looks for a place far from the big windows.

Everyone's on the staircase, sitting down, very prim and proper, talking things over and forecasting and flaunting their respective information and education.

Between them they know it all, but each knows better than the rest.

My father's sitting by himself, in the dining room.

Shows no signs of change.

Speaks with his usual tone of voice, a bit sardonic.

Says, while overhearing conversation on the staircase:

"There's gonna be a whole lotta *cajol* from here on out."

And with a glance and a slight movement of the head he signals in the direction of the stairs, from which a wall is separating us.

He smiles.

And me, I go back upstairs thinking of *cajoles* from here, from down there, from the jungle, from Mexico City, from the entire country, from Central America and from the rest of the world.

The little word is used a lot around these parts.

Cajol: A Tzeltal word comprised of *c'ajc*: heat, and *jol*: head. Hot head.

Two minutes without gunshots.

18:04 The streetlights come on.
Shoot-out continues.

18:13 Silence.
Night has fallen.

18:18 Geckoes, geese and gunshots.
I can no longer see.
Just a little clearing in the cloudy sky.

18:20 The houses have their lights off.
Gunfire ceased.

18:21 Another burst of machine-gun fire!
A truck comes down the street at full speed.
The rattling of sub-machine guns and machine guns furiously begins again.

18:24 Gunfire continues.
Nearby small-arms fire.
The dead street.
Almost total darkness.
Crickets.

18:27 Another hair-raising thud.
Comes a rain-like wind that violently shakes the clumped palm grove that's grown with impunity on the upper patio.
The royal palm wily growing in productive terrain, surrounded now by automobiles.
Will it rain?
There's a single star in the cloudy sky.
Another tremendous explosion!
Yet another!
The whole palm grove shakes.
The wind is cold.
Through the window I see two more stars.

But here I no longer see: I can scarcely write and, nevertheless, mustn't turn on the light.

Another violent reverberation: it shakes internally but I'm beginning to get used to it, and recover quickly.

I close the curtains. It's

18:30 Nothing: silence.

18:47 Light in the park.

There've been no shots fired.

But now they let loose: eight small-caliber rounds!

Carmelino yells for Eric to shut his door.

Eric was sitting on the doorstep of his house, looking toward the street.

The church towers jut skyward, framing the illuminated clock.

18:52 Silence since the last entry.

Five small shots like .22-caliber.

An intense blue space seems to have encroached upon the clouds.

Through that hole you can see, complete, the constellation of Orion.

19:10 Nearly 20 minutes of crickets and silence.

19:37 Two startling thuds behind the church.

Before that, just silence.

19:43 The blessed aroma of night jasmine wafts up to the inner terrace.

I've stayed behind here, alone, contemplating the stars.

I write by the light of a street lamp that shines from aunt Flor's house.

It passes over the foliage of orange trees and bougainvillea.

Spills a little light upon these pages.

19:57 Machine-gun fire resurfaces.
Brief.

20:10 Another short shoot-out.

20:34 My children call.
They're worried within reason: without panic.
We give them information as objectively as we can.

20:49 From town hall a billow of smoke keeps rising.
Seems longer by night.
Denser, amid the sky's partial clarity and the streetlights.
The houses remain in darkness.
As if we'd all agreed upon it.
In the sky you can see the two Ursas and the Great
Southern Triangle.
There's been no gunfire.

20:57 Three scattered gunshots near the church.
It's confirmed they freed the prisoners from the
CERESO,[47] in San Cristóbal.
It's rumored that the dead here now number more than
50.

23:15 At about nine, we had coffee with pan coleto[48] almost
in the dark.
Conversed.
There're 25 of us in the house.
25 points of view.
"It was necessary."
"There's a lot of poverty."
"The central government has been looting our state for
hundreds of years."
"These murderers have combat experience."
"Nobody kills unarmed people in cold blood like these
damned people did."
"Indians are very lazy."
"They've gotten very uppity."

"There's racism."

"There's no equal opportunity."

"He who works, possesses."

"There're lots of rich Indians."

"There's no longer any land to parcel out."

"A lot of foreign people have come."

"There's injustice."

"The priests have stirred up hatred."

"No to weapons."

"That liver-lipped Cárdenas."

"Old Sam."[49]

"The Maoists."

"The Bible in Tzeltal."

"We've built this town by working."

"Nobody's given us anything for free."

"We all work from sun up to sun down."

"They take away our petroleum, our fruit, our honey, our livestock."

"We're first in the production of corn, beans, coffee."

"The lazy bums want credit for everything."

"It's easier to organize people to kill than to produce."

"All the productive ranches the Indians invade become dens of poverty: that's how San José is."

"Yeah, but where'd the weapons come from?"

We saw the ECO News "special report": it said nothing about the confrontation here.

Nobody knows anything.

Four hours of intense and continuous and one hour of sporadic gunfire.

There're probably many dead.

How many?

Perhaps we'll know tomorrow.

More gunshots now.

Loud ones.

What'll happen to the hostages?

They've probably barricaded them in.

And the wounded?

How many on each side?

How they upset the family, the presidential candidates' statements.

Everybody, in the house, rebuffs Aguilar Talamantes, Madero, Cárdenas, Colosio, González Torres, Marcela Lombardo and Cecilia Soto.

They don't know what's happening here but they make statements, smile, seek votes, market their brand, make political capital out of blood.

That's how the press will be in a few days.

There've been scattered shots.

23:54 And the gunfire continues.

The marketplace, the library, the local Conasupo, the radio station, the neighboring houses: that's where they are, according to phone rumor.

They say the guerrillas have taken over more houses: have gotten into occupied houses.

It didn't rain.

There's a profound silence beneath the waning moon.

Dogs bark in unlighted houses.

A soothing gust of night jasmine rises.

Suddenly, it seems like all this hasn't happened.

23:57 Three shots.

3 JANUARY[50]

7:07 The first gunshots: three.

Television reports about the kidnapping of Absalón Castellanos.

The battlefield appears submerged in mist.

It's always like that in Ocosingo: the valley's surrounded by imposing hills to the west, to the north and to the east.

It opens to the southeast, towards the second valley.

The town.

A deep pool of mist, generated at night by the heat and humidity of the tropics.

From the church on back you can't see a thing.

The mist accumulates along the Virgin River bed.

That's how it is every day.

The view clears up from eight o'clock on.

By nine, at the very latest, all is transparency.

"It lifted already," is the common expression.

7:12 The first startling bang to begin the day!

7:30 The government secretary, Rafael González Lastra, nervous and with a frankly idiotic speech, wastes his television minutes broadcasting nothing more than the habitual vacuousness of official speeches, typical of the moonlighting civil servant to whom all political talent was denied.

Blather and blather and blather.

Condemnatory, moralistic, subjective, with an elementary-school chauvinism.

"What an idiot!" Aura says.

"What a moron!" Dora says.

"*Such* a foolish old man!" says don Rodulfo, my father.

They're airing news about dead bodies and destruction in Altamirano and Margaritas. Many dead policemen.

There's neither army nor police in Altamirano.

On TV utterly second-rate functionaries have appeared.

Why doesn't Elmar Setzer show his face, why doesn't Patrocinio show his face, why doesn't Salinas show his face?[51]

Why do they arrange for this man to speak, the one we just saw, so clumsy and so ill-informed?

I go to the terrace.

From the church on back, the town continues sunk in mist.

We've heard the government's offering dialogue.

But the EZLN declared war.

8:03 I look out at the street: a tiny group on the corner.

8:20 I had fruit and coffee, and have returned to the street. Lots of people.

I go down to the corner.

They say there're piles of dead people over by the market.

That the guerrillas are already surrounded.

That there're also townspeople among the dead.

That many guerrillas were leaving throughout the night.

That they were escaping along the creek bed, taking advantage of the manhole that crosses the beltway.

They were leaving along that route from the market area and "all you could hear was splish-splashing along the little stream. They were going downstream, toward the big river, and from there to the hill. Many were wounded."

The Army's patrolling town.

They say they detained two rebels and "they're giving them a good beating."

That more guerrillas arrived by night but could no longer enter because the soldiers made circles of protection around town.

That 10,000 soldiers will be deployed from the nation's capital.

A little old lady with silver-gray hair says: "Thank God they already killed some of them. It'd be good if they dropped a bomb on them in the market, to finish them off all at once. They came in for the kill first, and he who lives by the sword..."

Sweet little old lady.

They report that the mayor of Altamirano is hiding here.

That the police patrols, in Altamirano, were sprayed with bullets and set on fire afterwards, along with the policemen inside. And not all of them were dead.

But there they died: roasted.

That the shrieks of pain were heard all over town.

8:25 "The cannon's resonant roar" grows stronger.

Arístides Trinidad informs me that, according to César Cruz, there're about 150 dead bodies down below.

From both factions.

"But the soldiers won't let people go see."

"Because there're still a lot of guerrillas, holed up in houses."

The firing below grows worse and, as it worsens, the group dissolves.

I go back home.

Ascend to the solitudes of the inner terrace.

How many hummingbirds there are in the orchard!

The view over by the airfield begins to clear up, the combat zone.

Things like this I've heard on the corner:

That don Enrique Solórzano and the hostages escaped yesterday when the Army arrived.

That the Army rescued them miraculously.

That doctor Talango has disappeared.

That day before yesterday the guerrillas asked about the house of Fernando López, the mayor.

Nobody gave them information.

They just told them "downtown."

The guerrillas responded that they were going to burn the whole of downtown if they didn't give them information.

Nobody told them anything.

That one woman was begging and pleading, teary-eyed; "Don't tell them I work at the Prosecutor's Office... please!"

"Ah, must've been la Lucha."

"And what's la Lucha do there?"

"She's a secretary."

And the little group's members laughed.

But the woman's fear was real.

9:04 They say the Army ordered 1,100 pounds of tortillas. They weren't going to open the tortilla shop today but, at the Army's request, they opened and are doing business.

Some white flags are beginning to be seen on the street.

The Army has directed that those who come outside should do so with said flags.

9:33 We're sick and tired of being cooped up in the house. Look for things to do.

I sweep and prune the garden.

My sister roasts coffee.

The nieces and nephews grind grain with a hand-cranked mill.

The magnificent aroma floods the spaces.

We rehab the old kitchen stove because the gas is about to run out.

Four violent thuds sound in the northwest part of town.

9:58 On the pharmacy roof (a "modern" yellow building that seriously disfigures the landscape of downtown rooftops) there's a group of soldiers with a machine gun in place, aiming toward the market or the library.

At first you really couldn't tell if they were helmets or caps, but the binoculars pinpoint the image: they're helmets.

10:06 Loud bangs in the northwest.

It worries me: it's very close.

10:17 Another thud in the north, at the Yajalón exit.

10:23 Cross-fire.
Heavy fire.

10:29 More mighty explosions.
Bazooka and machine-gun fire.
Small-caliber rounds right near the house.
Low-impact gunfire in the southwest.
Gunshots continue very near here.
Two blocks away or less.
They get closer.

10:44 Shots on the corner.
I look out the medical office window.
A gate is opened near the highway.
A green pick-up truck goes out and descends at full speed.
A jeer: "Don't get yourself killed! Kill! Kill!"

11:14 Airplane noise.
Loud, but never appears.

11:15 Mario, my brother-in-law, calls from Tijuana.
Saying that the gringo news on CNN has shown heavy artillery among the guerrillas.
That the local Televisa news is too funny for words compared with what they're broadcasting there.
That the news team CNN sent is the same one they sent to Iraq to cover "the mother of all battles."

11:21 The plane continues flying overhead, but can't be seen.
Yes: there it is now: there're three.
You can hear an enormous number of shots, puny, harmless, against the planes.
The air flotilla circles above the town.

11:36 The planes are still there.
Firing in the north.
Very close by.

The day is hazy but the sun burns.
A light breeze is blowing.

11:45 Loud thud.
Two more.
Another and yet another.

11:47 Another loud bang.
In the house they say that, actually, the Ladino hostages escaped but that there's no sign of Doctor Talango.

11:49 Another furious explosion.

11:50 Once again the aerial flotilla, which disappears in the direction of Altamirano.

11:52 The flotilla returns and flies over the town in indefinable patterns.

Countless small-caliber shots are heard.

12:07 Fighter planes: transparent cockpit canopy and some kind of tank underneath.

12:32 Bullets nearby.

12:44 Three loud thuds.
Long silence.
Five thuds now.
Sound of a helicopter we can't see.
I follow the sound: it appears in the sky now.
Green and brown camouflage.
Flies over the valley.
From the terrace I see Miss Angela, our neighbor, washing clothes.
Doña Josefina, her mother, is preparing food.

Carlos Cisneros, whose house was about to burn down, looks, with his little boy, at the flight of the helicopter, from a door at don Beto Ruiz's house.

Three gunshots are heard over by the church.

12:58 Miss Angela goes out to sweep her sidewalk.
Collects the trash and sets fire to the papers.
"People are such slobs!" she says to herself.

13:02 Once again, the street has remained empty.
Shots in the southeast of town.
Carlos Cisneros goes down toward his house.
I see him go down and an image from elementary school comes to mind: there was excitement because "there's gonna be an ass-kicking after school."
Carlos and Fernando López Solórzano would fight: the Sparrow Hawk against the Fledgling.
What could Fernando have done?

13:04 Three gunshots behind the church.
Another, another, another.

13:08 Nine shots: seven all together.

13:20 Three men passing by with white flags.
One of them: "Why, the fuckers, do they come wage their guerrilla warfare here in town, when there's so much hill country?"

13:22 Another hair-raising explosion toward the northwest, followed by a small-caliber barrage.
13:30 Intense bursts of gunfire behind the church: machine guns and sub-machine guns.

14:35 Television news.
Salinas speaks.
Offers dialogue.
They don't at all mention that the EZLN declared war.

"Poor president: his big ears must've been burning," my father says.

14:45 González Lastra calls in to *24 Hours* and, with his drivel from this morning, is yapping the same idiocies but reconfirming and accentuating his ineptitude.

"It's because he's from Tabasco, that guy, but because he's González they brought him on the air," says one of my sisters.[52]

And the good gentleman wastes time, obfuscates, lies, confuses.

Faced with the hounding of Zabludovsky *fils*,[53] he states that the armed men number no more than 400.

Nobody tells this poor man anything?

15:00 Twelve helicopters fly over the town.

What a sound.

Apocalypse Now!

Some fly very low.

Come dangerously close to the market.

From all over town they shoot at them with small arms.

That means there're lots of rebels in unoccupied sites or houses... and not just around the marketplace.

At home, everybody runs and hides in the same old places: my mother's bedroom and the hallways.

There're protective walls there.

You can feel the wind of peril.

The thundering fire continues abundant.

You can hear small-arms fire against the helicopters. Pablo, with the binoculars, reports that the helicopters have machine guns in place and have no doors.

"Have you noticed that, every time you go out on the terrace, shots are fired?" my sister points out.

It hadn't escaped our attention.

They're not shooting at us because we'd have noticed already, but they are shooting.

I test the theory: gunfire!

Duck and go back, doubled over, to the hallway.

"Just a coincidence," my wife says, and takes two steps toward the terrace: once again, gunshots!

Enough... just in case, better not to go out on this terrace.

You can see the same thing from behind the wall.

I make a look-out post from partitions.

15:12 Who can possibly be shooting so close by?

A few minutes of calm.

Detonations are heard over by the church and Port Arturo.

The planes' noise continues.

The helicopters fly over again.

My nieces and nephews count 15.

I only manage to count 12.

15:15 Another formidable explosion reverberates in the northwest.

Another, like a loud bomb blast, which we heard a few yards away.

Almost on the patio.

Terror among us all.

The planes' noise continues.

We break through the paralysis and stick our heads out: nothing on the patio.

I go up to floor above: go to my observation point.

Nothing in the neighboring houses.

Nothing in the streets that I can manage to see.

Where'd that thud come from?

We heard it right here.

The family, reunited by fear, continues speculating.

"Those kids from this Zapatista army are children of the ETAS and CEBETAS."[54]

"They just established their residential area and already they want paved roads, electricity, water, good pastures, nice houses, satellite dishes."

"They have a right to all that."

And I think of how my town had no vehicular road till 1970, more than 400 years after its founding, and more than a century after don Juan Ballinas dreamed of a route that might unite central Chiapas with Tabasco.

We had decent electricity 20 years ago.

The highway to Palenque is still bad.

"But the young people of today were fed up already."

"And what are they fed up with if they've never had to suffer or build up the town?"

15:27 There's been calm.
Some of us are in the dining room.
There's activity in the kitchen.

15:37 Plane.
Another unsettling bang.
Two.
Exchange of gunfire below.
More ruckus towards the southeast.

15:41 Another brutal thunderclap!
Controlled fear from everyone in the house.
They sound like bombs.
But you can't see smoke, or flames, or anything else.
Only the horrifying roar which makes one think the town will be blown to bits.
We all take shelter on the bottom floor.
Loud gunshots, nearby, large-caliber.
Against the plane, I suppose.
Against the planes, three of them, which zoom violently flying very low.

15:50 The telephone.
Oscar Wong is calling, from Mexico City, to show heartfelt support.[55]
There seems to be extensive information in the city.
Another startling reverberation.
My mother is deeply affected.

They take her to her room.
My brother takes her blood pressure.
Her right arm hurts.

15:56 A nearby shot.

16:07 Isolated shots.
Loud impacts near the marketplace.
Nobody on the street.
The afternoon becomes cloudier.
A slight breeze is blowing.

16:09 Loud gunshots to the northwest.
The roosters.
The blackbirds.
The whispering of the wind.
The bougainvilleas, the coyol palms, the plantain leaves,
the diminished orange trees.

16:12 Another gunshot in the southwest.

16:14 Another shot in the same direction.

16:36 We already ate.
We tried to institute rationing but my mother firmly
opposed it.
"There's so much stuff and all the orchard hens are there.
God won't want this to continue very long."

16:53 Comes a helicopter and the barrage of small-caliber
gunshots.
Very close by and in the middle distance.
And from all four points of the compass.

17:00 Rain threatens.
A beautiful rainbow crowns the field of battle.
The blue hills blurred with the coming rain.
What a strange sensation.

Death hangs its hammock underneath the rainbow.
A bit of sun in the hills on the right.
The helicopter comes.
Passes over the house, very low.
No shooting, yet.
It flies over by the marketplace.
Goes off in the direction of the second valley.
Nobody shot this time!
The rainbow's right arm's still there.

17:12 A little while ago we were having coffee.
Suddenly Pillita's startled: "There's a man on the water storage tank! In a blue guayabera shirt!"
Everybody's shaken up.
"He's got a pistol in his hand!"
"Or a grenade! Something metal!"
We spy him from several different points.
He is, to be exact, inside our house: up on the water storage tank which the municipality constructed, taking a piece of land from us.
The man's still there, looking out over the horizon.
Too trusting.
Can he be an acquaintance?
"He's a guerrilla!"
No.
Have to see him close up.
"Don't go out!"
"He dropped something in the tank!"
"Poison?"
We get closer.
Pablo Jr., Charo, Luis go out.
Speak with him.
He wasn't a guerrilla: he's a waterworks employee.
What he had in his hand wasn't a pistol: it was the big padlock that the tank's locked with.
"It's just that nobody's seeing to the water. Only me. If I don't take care of the tanks not even what little water there is will be running."

17:17 Flocks of herons pass by toward their usual tree on the Virgin River.

All the valley's herons go there to sleep.

A single, colossal tree with immense white flowers.

They arrive in flocks, little by little, over a period of an hour and a half.

From every corner of the valley.

Just when it seems not one more will fit, a new flock arrives and perches on the branches.

Yet another flock. And another, and another, taking advantage of the last ray of sun.

Guadalupe and I discovered that tree last year.

We beheld the marvel from atop Shish bridge. On December 30 we took our friend, the young photographer Alejandra Villela, there.

We passed through "some thick vegetation, full of pernicious fauna" and that's why we arrived late.

The sun was already setting.

We managed to see the spectacle with binoculars, from far away and for only a few minutes.

There's nobody on the street.

In the corridor of a house up the way, past the highway, there's a group of men squatting.

"Ardentia of dogs" on the corner.

Two dogs mating and the rest trying to mount the female, with the male's consequent howls of pain: a big black dog, with paws like talons: el Capirucho.

"Happy are the mongrel breeds who have no fear of war."

17:20 Don Edgar Robledo Santiago calls,[56] asking whether we're having problems leaving town.

I thank him for his kindness, and tell him I hope we may be able to before the 7th.

We brought the car along with us, and have to be in Mexico City on the 10th.

17:25 Mauricio Flores calls from *El Nacional*.

He's doing a survey of writers.

Asks me about the letter that the Chiapas Prize winners signed proposing dialogue.

I give him my opinion.

18:30 They say there're dead bodies around Ramiro Ruiz's house.

That Lupe Cabrera died on the patio of his house.

Someone shot him.

18:45 Two small .22 shots.

18:51 Two more.

19:03 Televisa calls, "on behalf of Mr. Zabludovsky."

The reporter's name is Ana Cristina Peláez.

I give her the information I have.

We talk for a long time.

They record the Declaration of War, which they have systematically omitted.

Will they air it now?

19:59 There goes the electricity!

Blackout all over town.

Anxiety among us all.

I finish my talk with the reporter.

We scour the view from the second floor.

There's no electricity and not a single lit candle is visible, nor oil lamp, nor kerosene lamp.

20:00 My sister Dora talks with her friend Concha Solórzano.

The guerrillas got into her house last night.

12 of them.

"Since we have a chapel to Baby Jesus the Founder, they were praying there. They stayed there all night."

The Army drove them out in the morning, but there're lots of them who've invaded occupied houses.

§

22:30 We've gone through a spell of flailing anxiety and abundant fire.

Just when all seemed calm, and we'd already internalized the blackout, the shooting broke out.

It was about 8:30 at night.

There was fear among the whole family.

All of us cooped up in my parents' room, which is the one in the middle, between the medical office and Aura's bedroom, to the north; and the hallway, the bathroom and the kitchen to the south.

To the east lies another hallway and the living room, then the citron tree patio.

The west is the most vulnerable part: a large picture window which looks out over the corridor and the palm tree patio.

In this room my sisters, their husbands and their children are now.

In Aura's room are aunt Maga with her two Pablos and niece and nephew Isabella and Arturo, who are studying in San Cristóbal and live with her.

The firefight lasted roughly five minutes that seemed eternal.

In the darkness came a call from Juan Domingo Argüelles.[57]

We gave him some instructions for our children just in case communication is interrupted or in case something happens to us.

Afterward, Enrique Aguilar called.[58]

He's been looking out for our children, and will visit them tomorrow.

He calms us down and we deeply appreciate it.

Josie also called from Mexico City.

Mario spoke from Tijuana.

After the gunfight, we got ready for bed.

In the dark.

Mattresses were arranged on the floor of the best-protected room.

The children slept under their grandparents' bed.

Children and adults are one single fear.

My parents are the ones who exhibit the calmest demeanor.

When everyone was situated, I served coffee to uncle Mario and uncle Rodrigo, and accompanied them to their rooms crossing the upper storey patio.

On the way back I stopped for a moment beneath the palms: silence and crickets.

The bats that nest in these plants and some gun shots in the surrounding area scared me off.

In the darkness we bolted doors and windows, more for psychological than for physical protection.

The house is protected by high concrete walls towards Avenida Central, but is vulnerable over by Primera Sur, which overlooks the orchard.

If the rebels want to get in, they'll get in.

And if the Army wants to come in after them, they will.

I think about that and know there's nothing more that can be done.

My wife and I have decided to sleep in our usual room, on the second floor.

In the end, only the Goddess' will will be done.

4 JANUARY[59]

7:15 The first gunshots, although throughout the night, while half asleep, I thought I heard others.

The lights never came back on, and we now awoke without phone service.

Until last night, calls were coming in but weren't going out.

Today, nothing: line's dead.

Water's getting scarce.

7:32 Heavy gunfire in the northwest.

You can hear it over by the highway.

Also around the school.

Thuds continue, muffled, from heavy weapons.

Now along the river and over by the school.

Once again, tension.

Roosters crow and birds sing.

Whistling sound of blackbirds.

The gunshots cease.

It's 7:45.

7:51 Another shot.

7:54 And another, over by the school, small caliber.

A loud one along the river.

Two more.

I mean the town river, two blocks away, not the Virgin River.

You can't see anyone in the street.

There's no electricity, no tortillas, no telephone.

A few women pass by, hugging the wall, headed toward the tortilla shop.

Due to the power outage, there are no lights on at the tortilla shop, but they are selling Maseca.[60]

8:00 A loud shot over by park.

8:11 Two more over by the school.
Another one, very loud, along the river.
Today, we would be roofing our house. That little house we began building seven years ago. We've planted so many trees in that territory with the privileged view. We were excited about the second-floor gabled roof. The framework was ready. It seemed we could almost see it.

8:21 Gunfire in the southeast.
At this hour, you can't see a thing for the mist.
My wife goes to Carmelino's store; he'll sell us canned goods.
"Everything's running out already," he reports.

8:24 Sounds like helicopters or planes.

8:30 A whooshing sound like a very large projectile slices through the air from north to south.

8:32 A helicopter you can't see continues flying overhead.
More shots.
Dora and my wife succeeded in getting two boxes of merchandise.
There's no electricity.
Gas for cooking is running out.
We return, with gusto, to life the way it used to be: uncle Rodrigo shucked corn and made a fire in the old kitchen.
Guadalupe and I pick the husked corn.
Genner goes and gets the big pot.
Dora puts it on the fire.
In a while we'll be drinking home-made pozol.[61]
In the orchard, there's a full corn crib, and a small cellar with firewood.

There's sugar, salt and bags of beans.

Sacks of coffee.

The house is always provisioned, given the number of its inhabitants.

And we all enjoy manual labor, always.

The productive household.

From the ranch they bring in 50 liters of milk per day.

My mother sells half of it to aunt Flor's cheese shop, and the rest is sold here.

There's always enough left over to make cheese, cottage cheese, butter, cream, yogurt.

But Alfredo, the cowherd, hasn't come for three days.

He lives with his family on the ranch.

"And el Alfredo? Think he ran off with the Zapatistas?" asks Pillis.

"Aw, that guy's a bona fide coward. As long as he's not on maneuvers, he doesn't get involved. He's such a good-for-nothing that, so as not to have to carry a rifle, he probably told them to hand that ranch over to him when the war's over," my mother retorts.

Paca and Arturo sweep the garden paths and collect the trash.

9:25 The waterworks employee who startled us yesterday returns, and says the Army is firing salvos in order to intimidate people.

Says that Lupe Cabrera hasn't died.

Says he's been moving around all over town, on account of the water, and that he hasn't seen any dead bodies.

I sincerely hope so.

But how to believe him?

Adán Sánchez gave us the news of Lupe's death, and could hardly have been misinformed: his wife is the niece of the presumed deceased.

9:47 Paca whitewashes the trees: well, one tree.

I show her how, supervise her.

Angelica, Arturo, Karen, Teté, Oswaldo and Amber all shell green beans: take them out of the pods.

Put the empty pods in one little basket, and the peas in another.

Such is life in these valleys.

There's always something for everybody to do.

My sisters and my mother make breakfast.

There are still 25 of us in the house.

9:50 Four television and press vehicles pass by.

In the kitchen it smells like fried plantains.

People in the street: "The soldiers won't let anybody get close, only journalists."

They say they killed Uvelio Rosales.

Pilla and Dora go to the tortilla shop to get Maseca: there's a very long line and lots of news.

I ask uncle Mario to accompany them with his dolly, in order to bring back the bags of Maseca.

The kitchen smells like fried chili peppers.

In the street Capirucho, the big black dog with the claw-like feet, tries unsuccessfully to copulate with an itty bitty female.

There's been no gunfire, and there's calm in the street.

Lots of people go to the tortilla shop and chit chat on the corner.

Taking advantage of the lull, our neighbor Angela goes running to see her little sister, who lives at the Yajalón exit.

Arístides reports that there are wounded at the medical office, but the soldiers are protecting it.

Lots of people return with their purchases.

Chelo's tortilla shop is selling sacks of Maseca and cartons of eggs.

The tortilla shop is also local headquarters of the PRD.

Some say the guerrillas cut the electricity, and others say it was the Army.

No one's allowed downtown.

Doña Filomena, crying, comes to visit her daughter Toli, in the house across the street.

She's crying over the death of Lupe Cabrera, her nephew. Confirmed.

We wanted to re-emphasize the advantages of rationing, and encountered my mother's fierce opposition.

10:09 A bit of calm floats above the funereal town.

11:34 They say the corpses strewn about the marketplace, and especially those left up in the mountains are starting to be eaten by the dogs.

11:50 A helicopter flies over the populated area.
Shots are no longer heard.
A second helicopter appears.
They fly over the marketplace and Port Arturo, the area of heavy fighting.
Another helicopter, and another, and another, and another.
Eight altogether.
Camouflaged helicopters with machine guns and soldiers in plain sight.

12:20 A helicopter continues flying overhead.
The others flew off en route to Altamirano.
I think of all the interrupted activities.
My father hasn't been able to go to the ranch.
Don Pablo hasn't been able to take chicken feed to El Paraíso, nor eggs to San Cristóbal.
The bricklayers haven't been able to show up or finish the masonry: therefore, they don't get paid.
The workers haven't harvested coffee.
Alfredo has neither milked nor brought milk.
Edgar hasn't seen patients.
Isaías hasn't come to work.
Nor Maria, the maid.
Genner and Dora haven't taught class.
Luis and Mapi, either.

Oswaldo and Karen haven't gone back to high school in San Cristóbal.

Rosario and Domingo haven't returned to their medical school classes in Tuxtla.

The youngest children haven't been able to go to school.

Aunt Maguita hasn't been paid, and can't go back to San Cristóbal to check in on her house and her business.

We all do something around the house.

The least active are the ones from San Cristóbal.

Especially Luis and his children.

Likewise the younger Pablo.

They don't like to get their hands dirty.

They don't like to get their clothes dirty.

"That's just how people from San Cristóbal are: city folk."

And I notice they get bored more easily.

They don't know what to do with themselves.

They avoid the sun, the water, the dirt, the thorns and the ticks.

Their favorite areas are the living room and the bedrooms, the kitchen and the dining room.

Mingo studies Quiroz' anatomy all day.

Charo reads Valle Inclán.

It's marvelously sunny again.

We contemplate the horizon from the inner terrace.

And suddenly an ominous sign: vultures are circling overhead, high above the combat zone.

Between the clouds and blue sky, the small black whirlwind.

If that's how the vultures are, just imagine the flies.

12:30 A glance at the street: two kids with white flags arrive and knock at Elías and Lety's house.

13:03 Angela cries out to her mother: "Come see, mamma; look."

I go out with my wife.

Arístides and his son have come out, too.

Around the corner of the school a group passes by with a cedar coffin.

"There goes uncle José with that group," Guadalupe says.

Yeah, there he goes; what's going on?

We see Vitalia, my cousin, at Elías's house.

We call her. She tells us that Raymundo, Elías's youngest brother, has died.

"Going out to close his truck window."

That's what they came to tell us, a little while ago, the ones with the white flag.

There were no longer coffins in town, but Epigmenio Solórzano had had two made.

Benjamin, the carpenter, told me the story in September:

"Don José Arcadio came, and when he saw the boxes he said to me:

—And those... whose are they?

—They belong to Memo the teacher.

—Oh. And why two?

—One is for his aunt Salomé, and the other is for his grandmother.

—Ah, now that's clever! And what about his box?

"Don José got mad! Well, sure: doña Carmelita is his mother!"

I think about doña Carmelita, my godmother, who turned 100 in 1993. She's still sharp as a tack. Local radio interviewed her on the occasion of her 100th birthday. She lived through the Mexican Revolution and the Pinedist revolt. She had the Cardenist agrarian movement to deal with. She's been witness to these lands for 100 years. To the question of what changes she witnessed in people in all these years, she replied: "How young people these days no longer like to work... now they want everything done for them. They don't know how to go on foot or horseback anymore They only want cars. They no longer cultivate good crops. They want borrowed money just to plant."

Truer words were never spoken.

And unpredictable life is carried away from young Raymundo Penagos in one of the little old ladies' coffins. I met him as a boy. I hadn't seen him again until 10 years ago. Bachelor, still. Now, they tell me, now he was married and a family man. Today he's dead. Some think it was the guerrillas: "Because he helped pick up the policemen's corpses." But anything's possible: bullets from the soldiers or from the insurgents.

The brute fact of the matter is that he's dead.

13:30 There's a strange calm beneath the intense sun.

Pellucid air beneath a strikingly blue sky.

So much apparent peace in the resplendent valley!

What a lovely mirror the sun is for the sprawling valley, I once wrote.

And in that refulgent verdure death become intoxicated.

Death swilled, yesterday and the day before, its thick red wine.

13:40 Far from the vultures, which seem to have lessened, not even a fly is buzzing in the town air.

I don't see a single movement in doors, patios or windows.

See ranches in hill skirts of blazing greenery.

More intense dense patches of oaks and pines.

And behind this first green mountain range, the greater mountain range of intense blue.

To the right, the abrupt rib rack as if hacked away suddenly: the gateway to El Paraíso, at the entrance to the second valley, now overpopulated with co-ops and shanties and new residential subdivisions and basic necessities and redeemers ready and willing to carry us off to heaven at the point of a bayonet.

"All the world's evils come from us mattering to one another," says Pessoa.[62]

And I let this thought fly into the midday air.

13:55 Short shootout.

Everybody in the house is on alert.

I look out at the street: again, nobody.

14:05 The sun shines through the garden foliage and lights up the trees whitewashed by my little niece.

"We were always so happy in this town!" says my mother, who has worked every day of her life from five or six in the morning till ten or eleven at night.

She's always doing something.

Always, or almost, she has help in the kitchen but is in constant motion.

"There's never any shortage of things to do" for anybody.

And she serves milk, sets the table, orders breakfast, dinner, supper, dispenses pills, gives injections, knows where the saw is, the little hatchet, the pliers, the padlock, the darning needle, the pack needle, her grandson's little saddle, the lawn mower, the key to the ranch, the newspaper clipping.

Knows where the hens' corn feed is, the snap peas, the butil beans, the butter dish, the jute sacks, the cattle salt, the scale for weighing coffee, the paraffin lamp, the medicines, the steel broom, the flax, the roll of twine, my Salvadoran hammock, the rucksack filled with limes, the lady finger bananas.

Knows how many chicks hatched, how many speckled hens there are, how many cows are milking, what size mammy apples grow to. Knows whether or not the cinnamon or allspice is dried, when to plant and what time to harvest the chaya plant, how geese brood, how long it takes for puppies to be born, when our dog Capirucho is in heat, when it's safe to eat pacayas.

And the names of all the flowers in her immense garden.

And where the toronjil is planted and where the leeks, where the cilantro and the guaán plant, where the parsley, the mustard plant and the granadillas.

And everybody asks her everything.

And we tell her don't get up, don't bother, don't bend over, do stay put.

But she does not stay put, does get up, does bend over, does continue to make a fuss, so that everything may run smoothly in this enormous family, in this big house, in this heretofore so small town where "we'd been so happy until now."

Beneath this sky where, at 14:14 on January 4, 1994, another boom just rang out near the church.

14:47 On a battery-operated device we listen to the news about San Cristóbal: three billion pesos in damage to its City Hall.[63]

They also report 35 dead and an undetermined number of wounded.

There's talk of two dead officials and five Federal Army troops.

They say they collected rifles.

15:10 Another military helicopter flies over the populated area.

16:00 A group of soldiers on Lety's corner, where the guerrillas were before.

16:15 Electricity is restored.

The helicopter, once again.

The streets are still deserted.

Four Army trucks pass by.

17:14 There're soldiers on the roof of town hall.

They're chatting very casually.

Suddenly, a gunshot.

They duck, run, some bunching up around the machine gun.

Crouch.

Take their positions.

Then nothing: pregnant silence.

17:58 The sky takes on a rose-colored tinge above the strips of cloud beginning to form flush against the horizon.

Behind the central mass of the church, the only beautiful building that's been constructed in this town in 500 years, the layers of color follow one another thus: dark green in the hills, blue, white of low-lying clouds, pink of sky, gray clouds, white-ish higher above and a gray-ish blue in the canopy of heaven.

Wind sways the enormous royal palm tree I planted in the lower patio when my son Balam was born, 18 years ago.

18:11 The streetlights are on.

Calm in town: let's just say there's no gunfire.

Nobody knows anything about the dead.

In the yellow building, the pharmacy, soldiers on the roof.

At town hall, too.

On the Bodas de Plata Hotel roof, soldiers maneuver with chairs and mattresses and small tables: place them between the blue water tanks.

Here, in the living room, my nephews are watching television.

Uncle Mario is sleeping in his chair.

Didn't sleep well last night.

19:30 Nobody in the street.

Kissing sound of geckos in the garden.

Where've they been these days?

21:10 There's been sporadic gun fire.

Telephone line hasn't been restored.

My children must be worried.

22:00 A hundred dead some say, very few considering how many shots were fired.

How many projectiles, I wonder, have been used during these long days?

500,000?

A million?

More?

And who are the dead, I wonder?

The local boys, Tzeltal Mayans with rubber boots and small-caliber arms? Or their commandants, with high-powered weapons and impressive equipment?

The television images show only poor Indians.

It's painful, the thought of that young Tzeltal left for dead three days with three bullets in him.

I think about the cold of mornings, evenings, afternoons.

And about the gradual heat that changes to savage midday sun.

And about the dead lying nearby this youth who still can speak:

"They just left me here to die. The war's about to begin, they told me. I was going out to my corn field. They just dragged me here."

One day bleeding to death on the hard pavement.

And another day.

And yet another.

On the cold hard ground.

In his own blood.

Thinking who knows what.

Feeling who knows what.

Saying who knows what.

What are we going do with all this sadness?, my wife's eyes ask me, welling with tears.

I take her hands and squeeze them, long and tight.

We turn off the light.

5 JANUARY[64]

7:41 People look out apprehensively at the street.

The soldiers posted at the school signal that nobody should pass by, and begin rapid mobilizations.

Some women run.

My sister and my wife see them coming.

"Where do we go, for godsakes?"

We open the door for them, and they come in.

People run toward their houses slathered, almost, against the wall.

A man, a boy, two women run passing by.

"Better hungry than dead."

A plane flies over.

Six Army trucks come up, empty.

The situation calms down a bit.

The women leave.

7:55 No soldiers are seen at town hall, nor at the pharmacy, nor at the Bodas de Plata hotel, but they do seem to be at the Hotel Central.

The ones at the school signal that people can now pass.

Dora goes to the tortilla shop.

8:10 There the soldiers are, atop town hall.

One of them folds a reddish quilt.

8:20 Dora returns.

Reports that they buried Lupe Cabrera in the backyard of his house, because going to the cemetery was physically impossible.

Reports that la Chela, a woman who worked many years for our family, since back in my great-grandmother's day, laughed on hearing the shoot-out: "It was worse during the revolution."

8:28 Helicopters. The woman from the corner restaurant went all the way to the marketplace: the corpses are still there. "They're bloated now."

I join a group that's conversing on the corner.

They report that only two people could get to the cemetery for burying Raymundo.

They say Alfonso Cruz is wounded.

Let's hope to God that's not true.

The remark alarms us a little.

We agreed to meet him day after tomorrow in Toniná.

9:35 The use of white flags has become widespread.

The streets are embellished with little flags waving.

Some they've made from paper.

Others from plastic bags.

Anyway, the street looks pretty with the white fabrics.

The river of banners is swirling around the tortilla shop.

Lots of soldiers leave the school. They clear it already?

An Army ambulance comes down the street.

The driver and his partner.

Both armed.

10:10 My wife and I decide to go down, a bit apprehensively, to the town center. Arístides and his son will go with us.

Elías Penagos offers us a flag.

10:12 We pass between young and tired soldiers, unrecognizably affable.

The park, deserted, reveals the same disorder from day 2.

We arrive at the church.

Approach the corner that leads down toward the marketplace.

There're tons of people looking around, in a strange pageant of astonished, pallid facial expressions.

Everyone's whispering.

So much clothing lying around!

Mismatched garments, bits of fabric, blood stains, broken cables, bullet-ridden houses.

Three bullet-riddled stores: Commercial Hardware, Nichim Agroveterinary, Flores Shoe Shop.

"The guerrillas put up quite a fight here. In these stores and in the empty houses," says a man in a group contemplating the hundreds of bullet holes, of every caliber, upon these perforated walls.

I hear hushed voices.

Gaze upon the multicolored mess.

Scattered clothing.

Water gushes from broken tanks and runs out into the street.

I linger over that sensation: the sound of running water amid human babbling.

I look at the water tanks perforated by bullets.

The man continues recounting that a gentleman, don Amílcar, confronted the guerrillas from here.

"He was firing shots at them all by himself. And those bastards against him. Till he ran out of ammo, which lasted him only a little while, and he fled through the back yards. He took off running. Who knows where he is, but they didn't catch him. One thing's for sure: they busted into his house and destroyed everything. They stayed there. From there they were firing upon the soldiers. And the soldiers upon them, till they drove the guerrillas out. There was a double shoot-out. That's why the house ended up like that."

I listen and take notes.

My wife has gone on ahead, taking pictures.

A boy displays his collection of shell casings.

There're tons of people.

Broken cabling from XEOCH radio:[65] a tremendous tangle.

You can smell the stench.

I watch the vultures' flight.

Lots of rubber boots in a pick-up truck.

The foul odor increases.

We arrive at the marketplace.

A passageway: the multicolored mess: small display tables, pieces of blue, black, orange, red plastic; half-empty soda bottles; bed mats and cartons, all over the floor.

Three tennis shoes.

Pineapple leaves.

A young man, shirtless, dead in a pool of blood.

A dog noses around the blood.

A boot nearby.

People cover their noses, and scare the dog away.

Flies and nausea.

There, further ahead, another body.

I go out and make my way to the corner, toward the local market.

The local market: two rows of cement stalls, where the rebels fortified themselves.

They'd have seemed perfect as trenches.

There's subdued grief on the faces of the people gazing on.

A kind of anguish in their curiosity.

Jackets on the ground.

A wooden rifle, crudely carved, with a piece of hose in the barrel to simulate a muzzle, and a piece of wire rod inside the hose.

More rifles, almost identical.

Lots of rifles.

More or less primitive, but all made of sticks.

Some with oil paint.

Others with tar or shoe polish.

Clothes, pouches with blankets, ropes, backpacks.

The stench increases.

Two dead youngsters, bloating up amid their backpacks, in their black and brown uniforms, with their rubber boots on.

More clothes: brightly-colored shirts.

Tin cups.

A flash light in one of the dead people's hand.

A stack of bean tortillas.

Plastic bags of pinole.[66]

Balls of pozol falling out of a backpack that reads RAM ARMY.

Little plastic bags.

Fifteen feet away from these dead bodies a man opened his stall: took the lock off the storage unit beneath the concrete slab, took out the merchandise, and is selling tomatoes, avocados and potatoes.

And people are buying, because groceries are in short supply.

You can barely walk amid all the stuff lying around.

A bag of Maria cookies and a heap of white tostadas fall from one of the pouches.[67]

Another dead body.

And another, two stalls away.

And the pile of stuff extends for 50 yards, between the two rows of stalls at this zinc-roofed local market, which boasts the name of former governor González Garrido's wife.

10:35 Nine helicopters are thumping in the sky.

And on the ground these sardine cans, this barricade of blocks.

And more backpacks, more pozol, more Rayovac batteries, more yellow plastic canteens.

And a stick with a knife at the tip.

And blue-corn tortillas.

Behind the barricade there's a black briefcase, with bank notes and lots of coins, from back in the old days, which onlookers want to take their chances with.

A cartridge belt, hand made, sewn with a tarp needle, with bullet hoops made from hard plastic.

A man in a yellow T-shirt speaks: "The head honchos left in three trucks, around twelve o'clock. Down there, toward the jungle... here's where they left about 300 of the most fucked up guerrillas here. Just for cannon fodder."

This man's peace flag is a little white T-shirt, a child's.

More wooden rifles, carved with a machete.

Here these young bodies remained, as if positioned for sacrifice.

A handle, hard, as if made of sapodilla wood, with a machete tip: this certainly makes an impression: it's gracefully made, with great care; a solid and terrifying weapon if you were fighting hand to hand.

But what can this handicraft piece do in the face of end-of-century artillery?

I continue forward amid cans of chili peppers, boots and boots and boots and tortillas and plastic.

I cross the street: there's a man doubled over, dead underneath the wooden stall on the corner.

Among the things scattered about I see a Mauser bayonet from the days of the Mexican Revolution, rusty, detached, with a cord at one end, as if it had been tied to a stick.

And more jackets and jackets and jackets and tin cans and checkered shirts and poor little backpacks and boy's-sized machete sheathes and a box of Abuelita chocolates with the bars scattered all over the ground.

I imagine these youngsters sewing their cartridge belts of green burlap in a sunny corner of the jungle, under tall trees, on the bank of streams, near the Jataté River, beside their cornfields or on their coffee plantations, following the precise instructions of some guerrilla trainer, most likely urban, most assuredly college-educated, who wants to impose on us, by force of arms, *la furiosa esperanza*.[68]

Can one world view be worth a single human life?

A single life which may not be our own?

Be worth the life of this youth with black eyebrows and barely visible peach fuzz, black cheeks, and white teeth in his open mouth where now I see flies, and where maggots are beginning to squirm?

Here he remained, beside his stick rifle which has a small leather pouch so it can be carried.

Beside his backpack and his flash light.

Beside his red bandana and a pack of cigarettes, also red.

And the grim politicians will come spouting their rhetorical language: better to die on your feet than live on your knees.

Pure fraud, one voice will respond.

False dichotomy.

The poet will say, better *to live* on your feet.

And being on your feet all the time is exhausting.

Sometimes you feel like sitting down on a rock.

Or on a chair.

Or on a log.

Or lying down on a bed.

Or on the ground upon the sedge.

And why not: it also makes sense to get down on one's knees to kiss the thighs of the woman one loves.

Or to honor, each, his god.

And I find myself with my glasses all fogged up, about to cry *like a little girl*, as Sabines said.[69]

And my wife now goes on very far ahead, and I have to catch up to her.

10:55 A man asks for help taking an unexploded grenade out of his house. His name's Moisés Trujillo Morales. They introduce us and he informs me he was my brother Edgar's elementary school classmate.

He knows our family well, and we're pleased to meet him.

He introduces us to his son.

Is very worried because "that thing fell in his back yard. And there are family members around."

10:57 This is the manhole they escaped through. There's hardly room for one man but it's miraculously positioned here: allows for crossing the street without being seen and one can follow along the stream bed (here it's now waste water) and reach the open field, the big river, the hill, and salvation.

Arístides' young son calls us over to a recently plastered construction site.

Still has no floor: there's leftover framework and mortar on the unlevel ground.

We peek inside: a naked corpse, with its eyes half open, upon a framework table.

There's a jar of Nescafé, a big bag of cement mix, a container of juice.

And on the recently plastered wall, like a brutal red refulgence three feet long, the splattered blood.

We walk about this outer ring of recent construction.

In the small gullies that skirt the street, there's a long series of holes; niches in which a squatting man can fit, like defenses, like small trenches where the rebels took cover, from here all the way to the marketplace.

There're more than a hundred similar niches: the majority are shaped just for the body on the tall grass.

We arrive at don Enrique Solórzano's house: five burned cars (only the blackened frames remain) and two more autos with bullet-ridden glass.

Behind the broken windows you can see the disorder, the destruction.

There're six dead bodies at the street entrance, bloated, as if about to burst.

Black due to decomposition.

There's one with a cap on, his face completely blackened, his red bandana tied at the neck, the heavy-duty brown shirt over a blue T-shirt with white buttons, the pants black and the boots yellow, shiny, new.

"He'd just stolen them from Calzamoda," an onlooker says.

There's a big blood stain on his left knee.

He's got one arm raised, bent, with three fingers cocked and the index finger pointing at his head, like an expressive gesture.

And that face of such intense blackness.

He probably died face down.

Gravity collected the blood in his face and, long afterward, they turned him over.

This would explain that gangrene blackness.

Yet another: half his face was destroyed; isn't there, doesn't exist; in that half hollowed-out as if with a big spoon, the color white contrasts with the intense black of the other part.

At ten yards, the face in black and white seems like a harlequin.

At five yards you can discern the cavity, the missing half, extremely white.

From here, a yard away, the white seems to be roiling.

And is roiling.

It's a bunch of maggots.

And this *slow worm all along the soul* .[70]

More batteries close to the dead bodies.

Boxes of matches

I stop to look at that hand-made holster, those heaps of plastic, those jumbles of clothing, that slew of medications spilling out of a small backpack, those boy's-sizedmachetes.

Rifle cases, also hand-made.

And here, very near the dead bodies, extremely scrawny, the feet sticking up, the sharp beak, the long tail feathers, the plumage exceptionally black in the dust: a dead blackbird.

A bullet stopped it in mid-flight.

"Injun and raven, the law demands its life be taken," a racist refrain from the not too distant past used to go.

We take the road that leads to the cattle-breeders' association: very bullet-ridden but not burnt: at least not the building, nor the thatched roof: just furniture, saddles, ropes, stationery.

Sad calm.

We make our way toward the cemetery and toward the IMSS medical office.

The death stench follows.

We pass by don Uvelio Rosales' house.

Indeed, they killed him: there's the black mourning cloth, on the pink wall of his house.

We express our condolences to his oldest son.

He tells us:

"The shot entered his back and came out his chest. A bullet hole this big. When we went to seek help burying him, the soldiers detained us. They herded us into a truck, blindfolded us, took us up there by the highway and put us face down on the ground. Me, I showed my driver license but, rotten luck!, they find a damn quetzal on me,[71] one of those little souvenirs they give you when you travel. You're Guatemalan, you bastard!, they were telling me. No, here's my driver license, you can ask my boss, we were going to ask for help burying my father because they killed him. And they didn't believe me. My little brother, they made him sing the national anthem, good thing he didn't forget it from nervousness! That way, they let us go. We buried my father here in the yard. Since my brother-in-law's a carpenter, he made the coffin. We'll see whether or not they want us to dig him up later."

And Jesús Rosales continues:

"They killed Lampo Trujillo, too. Well, he was a little bit sick in the head. Since he really liked to sing, he used to come often. That night he was here keeping vigil over my father, all by himself. He left late, seems he was going to stay over at don Enrique Escandón's house. But, as he was passing the cemetery gate, they put a bullet in him. There he lay. The guy they used to call el Chesco, they killed him too. El Chémber's son-in-law. Him they got for running over to his nephew's house to bum a cigarette. He died of a bad habit."

We say goodbye.

Continue walking.

A gentleman comes along from Pequeñeces, aunt Julia and uncle José Trujillo's once beautiful ranch, later inherited by Chus, dead a few years since.

The man comes with his buddy.

They tell us that a guerrilla girl entered their house.

She changed clothes and told them that she had to get to Pamalá.

That in Patihuitz and Campo Alegre 2,000 guerrillas are gathered, ready to retake the town.

His buddy speaks:

"I have a truck and make trips down that way. Yesterday, the guerrillas took my truck from me in San Quintín. I came on foot all the way from down there. Those bastards won't be long now. We want to warn the feds, because those guys said they're coming in for the kill."

The men go downtown.

We continue toward the cemetery.

Pass by the house where Chesco's blood still remains.

On arriving almost at the bridge over the little creek situated just before the burial ground, they show us a hole in the pavement: a hole the size of a small plate.

"A bomb fell here," the kid showing it to us says.

"Must have been a grenade," Arístides says.

We're looking at this when a gentleman comes out his door asking us if we're reporters.

Me they see writing, and Guadalupe with her camera.

We make it clear to him that no, we're not reporters, just private citizens.

Introduce ourselves.

He invites us to see the state his house was left in.

We enter the patio.

He's a schoolteacher and also a gas distributor in town.

Shows us a truck with tanks full of gas.

Next a Nissan wagon, to the right of a Volkswagen.

Four paces ahead the hole from another grenade, in the center of the patio.

It's just like the one from the street.

But its violent aftermath is here, on one side of the wagon: we can see the four flat tires, and we count 34 perfectly visible holes.

"The wagon saved us. If it wasn't here, all the shrapnel hits the truck. And once the gas exploded, this would've been hell."

I see the fanning out of holes on the Nissan's doors.

Think of a falling honeycomb: on impact the wasps fly out.

So with the grenade: it falls and lets fly its lethal red wasps.

Some flew high: pierced the truck's exhaust pipes, above the tanks of gas.

The Volkswagen also reveals holes.

The idea quickly occurs that the grenade could have fallen between the vehicles and the house.

I approach the truck: It's tires are punctured, too!

We go out.

Jorge the schoolteacher shows us his metal entry gate: a bullet pierced a tube.

We arrive at the cemetery. Four trucks full of soldiers go down the beltway. Toward the southeastern ranches. Toward Toniná.

The cemetery manager appears: his name's Genaro.

Says they buried ten in a mass grave.

"Since they couldn't get in over here, they opened up a hole in the wall on that side. The hole's still there."

The soldiers.

Another grenade fell here: a cement peephole.

Lupe Pimienta lives next to the cemetery; she's Arístides' godmother.

They greet and she reports.

The soldiers made the hole.

"Because guerrillas were shooting over here."

And she points to a house opposite the cemetery: there's a trench of blocks on the roof.

Suddenly the street seems to have emptied.

No one's there.

We want to reach the medical office, 50 yards away, but nobody's there.

And farther along, nobody.

We return with a strange feeling.

12:05 Back at the corner; we head straight to the church.

We see, now, a few people.

We get within two blocks of the plaza.

On the corner, at Jorge Ordóñez' house, we run into Antonino and Armando Cruz, Alfonso's relatives: cousin and brother, respectively.

—What happened to Alfonso?—we ask—Is it true he's injured?

Antonino shakes his head.

His eyes are filling with tears.

—He left us. Today at 6:20 in the morning.

Armando leaves Jorge's house.

Condolences.

Heartache.

The field hands, ranchers with sunburnt skin and rough hands, shed their manly tears.

Now, day after tomorrow, we won't see Alfonso in Toniná. Never again.

Someone says, in the street, that the General Prosecutor's Office arrived.[72] The Federal Judicial Police.

12:28 We've returned home.

Before that, we stopped by to express our condolences to Alfonso's parents.

There, in the living room, the casket surrounded by four votive candles and flowers.

The mother cries, inconsolable.

There's worry and heartache.

Where to bury him?

Paperwork needs to be done, and there are no authorities in town.

Not even the mayor peeks his head in. "He's hiding beneath his wife's skirt," somebody said, a while back, in the marketplace: when people were showing concern because the corpses haven't been collected and an epidemic can break out.

Alfonso leaves behind a widow and children.

Last year he was very happy with his ranch's thatch roof.

Had a small restaurant for the tourists that visit Toniná.

The archaeological site is located in the vicinity of his ranch.

That's why he and Antonino were working as caretakers of the site, employed by the INAH.[73]

We've returned home through empty streets.

We would stop at every corner, take out the white flag, wave it around, then move on.

The air charged by high tension.

13:25 I'm writing in the garden.

Beneath the daggers of light slashing through the foliage.

A dazzling yellow bird atop a medlar tree: three yards away from me.

But it still reeks of death.

And there's no water.

And I have a strong urge to cry.

I go up to the bedroom.

My wife comes in.

Hugs me and cries intensely for several minutes.

Her crying gives me strength: protecting her breaks through my defenselessness.

I think of ranchers' hands, owners and workers: hands like earth, full of cracks, of tough calluses, accustomed to the machete, to the long hoe, to the pickax, to the hatchet; to making support beams, to driving fence posts, to gathering bundles of firewood, to splitting ocote pine; to planting cornfields, beans, squash, chili peppers; hands almost animal: more human for that very reason.

And I think about the well-groomed hands of the declarers, the signers of manifestos, of the innumerable lackeys.

14:43 Two military planes scissor through the sky.

15:21 Three helicopters, two camouflaged and one white, land in INI territory.[74]

The sun lights up the deserted town.

15:56 I go out to take the sad sun on the upper patio: cold sun.

16:05 A gunshot, more or less nearby, over by the highway.

16:52 I think about the little backpacks of green sackcloth, sewn with crude stitching.

And about the scabs, the puddles, the lines of dried blood, the dark color of the corpses.

I think about the naked man, with his eyes open, on the plank full of dried mortar, with his halo of blood, at the construction site.

17:53 A lazy afternoon goes by.

Icy air, even though there's sun.

Not a soul in the street.

The notebook, the ink pen, my urge to keep on writing, have all run out.

19:23 I backslide: Edgar treats me to a new notebook.

Three bombshells to the southeast.

The afternoon passed by in a tense atmosphere, beneath the splendidly blue sky.

The family's afraid.

My wife's been crying.

There's fear, grief, profound sadness.

Anxiety must be calling upon my children, although I warned them the telephone could be cut off.

The two Pablos are thinking of leaving for Palenque tomorrow, but aunt Maga doesn't want to.

It's a bit risky, but the Red Cross has extended a bridge of protection for those who want to skip town.

The route they think of taking to get to San Cristóbal is Palenque-Teapa-Pichucalco-La Tijera-San Cristóbal.

Lots of people will be leaving.

Especially those who came to spend the holidays with their family.

But many people will be taking their families with them.

My parents flat out reject the idea of leaving.

"This is our home and if it's our fate to die here, well so be it," my mother pronounced a while ago, at the suggestion of going to San Cristóbal or to Mexico City.

She's right.

And she's passionate.

We'll stay here.

The silence we perceived on returning from the cemetery was not unreal: news of the 2,000 guerrillas in Patihuitz, Pamalá and Campo Alegre had spread all over town.

That must have been why people disappeared from the streets.

At this point, I can say we were scared at the cemetery, faced with the suddenly deserted scene.

A while ago a man passed through the street and said the dead bodies were now gathered up.

Dora and her family will once again sleep here.

Her house is up the way, across the palm tree patio.

It wasn't just me: the wind is carrying, at times, gusts of death stench.

Night has fallen.

Once again there are stars.

Very cold.

23:15 An image has haunted me: when day is done, at the markets a great quantity of garbage remains amid the stalls: spoilage of lettuce, cabbage, carrots, radishes, fruit, rotten or bruised tomatoes, leafy greens with yellowish or brown spots. That's how the local market looked at a distance of 50 yards. Closer to, the image became clearer in such a way as to perturb soul: they were human bodies, bloody remains, broken bodies, black boots, green pants, little brown sweaters, dried blood, pools with black parts and deep red blood clots.

And that smell of slaughter that had attracted flies, dogs, vultures.

And reporters who will belch forth carrion tomorrow.

6 JANUARY[75]

7:00 A plane.

Throughout the night those brutal impacts of previous days were heard.

Far away, in the direction of the Jataté River.

8:00 The sky's absolutely clear.

Sun above the roofs and above the highest eastern hills.

The area where the Virgin River runs, behind the church, appears sunk in white mist, as usual.

Soon, without anyone noticing, the thick mist disappears.

It's cold, but today's sun seems different.

We'll see.

8:10 On my father's initiative, we make a sign to post on the entry gate: "There's no water or telephone."

The news has reported that life in San Cristóbal returned to normal already.

"But not here, and if the press is coming to town, like yesterday, it should be known that life here's still interrupted," is my father's argument.

There're people in the street.

Carmelino's doing business.

Since there're no classes, the nieces and nephews ask me for things to do.

I put them to work sweeping the patios because today we're going to take coffee beans out to dry.

While they're doing their chores I paint the cobbler's shoe repair stand red: a cast-iron foot, welded at a point that's been firmly nailed upon a base of solid oak, hatchet-carved. Once the iron's painted, I place the piece upon an oak half-trunk, about two feet high and just as wide.

There it stands against a white pilaster of the southern corridor.

A wartime homage to Joan Miró.

08:45 Now we take the coffee out to the patios.

There was moist coffee that was already getting moldy.

Although there's been good sun the past few days, it wasn't possible to take it out, on account of the shooting.

But now the piles are on the patios.

My father spreads it out with wooden rakes.

Uncle Rodrigo made a fire on the old kitchen stove.

There, my sisters will roast more coffee.

The two Pablos are set on leaving.

Aunt Maguita doesn't want to but won't let them go alone.

Pablo Jr. asked Toño's son to move his truck.

They've now moved it.

There's movement of cars on the patio.

Ready to leave.

I give Pablo Jr. my children's telephone number so he can tell them we're alright.

Our aunt and uncle's departure worries us a bit, but their minds are made up.

Since day before yesterday they began discussing it.

They want to take advantage of the convoy that will set out for Palenque today.

Aunt Maga's arm was very swollen last night.

My mother prepared her a poultice and today my aunt's arm appeared normal.

My mother dictates the recipe: five large mango leaves; one tablespoon of striped curare, split into pieces; a rib of purple agave; a big branch of marigold.

"Any old marigold," she adds, while I come away savoring the image.

"It's used for fomentations and for compresses, in inflammations. As hot as you can stand it."

09:20 All the patios are covered with perfectly raked coffee.

It's my father's job this time of year.

In the street white flags continue waving.

I now see them accompanying some women on bicycles and adorning a red Volkswagen.

09:24 "Hey, Carmelino, gimme my flag!" shouts one man from a group that just exited the store.

Ten people, forming a group, await their turn to go inside.

A dog barks at a man on a bike.

My wife brings me the most beautiful Brazilian cherry that she found in the garden.

A perfect waning moon bejewels the blue sky.

The children work together with their parents in roasting the coffee.

The heavenly aroma's now inundating the patios and the house.

The passengers are about to depart.

Don Pablo is a 77-year-old Spaniard who was a political prisoner under the Franco regime.

Was sentenced to 30 years in prison, of which he served six.

Now he's a pensioner of the Spanish government, and the husband of aunt Maga.

Pablo Jr.'s father.

El Paraíso belongs to them.

Don Pablo's tried everything there, on his 35 acres, his orchard, his natural spring and his spacious house.

"There're no reshponsheeble people anymore, nothing but thievesh," has been his catch phrase ever since I've known him.

At this point he'd started breeding chickens and producing eggs.

Finally got it right.

Everything was going well, but the war blocked his progress.

When will he be able to return to his Paradise?

Will he be able to?

I get along well with don Pablo: he's very cooperative and very daring and very naïve.

On day 2 he went down to the corner to chat with a group of Tzeltal guerrillas: "OK, but you guysh, whowhat do know avout Marxishm-Leninishm? Bee cause I know more tthan you. Bee cause I wash een thee Shpanish Theevil War."

"And how did they respond, don Pablo?" I ask him.

"No thing. Yesh, shir... yesh, shir... and I didn't kick tthem out of tthere."

"That's great, don Pablo. If you come across any Central Americans, how about if they enlist you in the ranks eh, commandant?"

With this recollection and with this dialogue we say our goodbyes.

Hugs for aunt Maga and Pablo Jr.

Good luck.

09:58 Calm has increased.

Some women come around selling pork and chicken.

In a house up the street they're slaughtering a pig: long, piteous squeals are heard.

"We're craving us some pork rinds now," says my smiling sister Dora as she passes.

In the store people report that the guerrillas holed up in some houses in Barrio Magisterial, a new development, for ISSSTE workers, that was constructed far from town, outside Pequeñeces.

That they carted off things.

10:05 My mother's crying because her sister left.

Aura's whining like a little girl: "She doesn't even cry that much over me."

A youngster reports that 12 cars left for Palenque.

Carmelino closes the store for a while: they're going to lunch.

When they finish they'll continue doing business.

Today I wanted to see how the mist disappears in the depression, but I forgot.

All clear already.

You can feel the absence of Aunt Maga, the two Pablos, Angelica and Arturo.

There're 20 of us left in the house.

10:22 The store opens again: the small door.

Shoppers enter one by one.

10:50 Edgar and Mingo play ping-pong, very lightheartedly.

Since they haven't brought milk from the ranch, there's no queso fresco.

But all the hard cheeses, held in reserve, that my mother sells as cheese for grating, are being consumed with gusto.

Even those are already running out.

This is a typical day in the valley: high and clear, cloudless, extremely blue, above the intense greenery.

The dazzling bursts of bougainvillea, the floral explosions, the swaying of plantain trees, fields of maize and palm trees.

But someone said a while ago that amid the *canchishal* thickets some dead bodies remain, abandoned to the dogs' jaws.

10:58 The helicopter returns.

Everyone in the street with their white flag.

A bannered peregrination to the tortilla shop.

They come see Edgar for a doctor's visit on account of diabetic crisis.

Inform us that one girl died.

They found Doctor Talango already.

He's dead, apparently since day two.

11:22 Four cars carrying civilians pass by towards Palenque.

Some with Veracruz license plates.

They say there're dead bodies near the agricultural technical institute.

The street has come to life.

Passing in front of me a young girl in a red T-shirt, with a low-cut neckline and big firm tits, very big for her stature.

She busts me staring at her.

Smiles.

There goes the young thing on up the street, "shakin' her rump real nyshe and jooshy," as we casually say, imitating Gabriel Vargas, in Mexico City.[76]

Sign of life.

Is Capirucho corrupting me?

I see two young Tzeltals coming.

They come up the street as if scared.

Are wearing clean and very wrinkled clothing.

As if recently changed.

Extremely tired.

Surely they were rebels.

Must have been trapped somewhere, in some house, and left only just today, taking advantage of the movement of people through the street.

Such fear in their faces, such concern.

They don't look at anybody.

Pass right in front of me, two paces away.

Speak but don't make eye contact.

New boots.

Like the ones that dead guerrilla had on.

They continue up the street.

Fare ye well.

In the crowd of shoppers some say they have rebels hidden in the church cellars.

"Or used to have, they must have helped them get out already."

My father insists, "how can they expect people not to revolt if they take so much away from Chiapas: petroleum, electricity, natural beauty, cultural riches, poetry, novels, archeological treasures, corn, beans, livestock, honey, shrimp, marvelous birds, research materials, timber.

"And they've exploited chicle gum base, sugar, rice, cotton, milk, cocoa, coffee."

"And here's the proof: there're no good roads, not even mediocre ones."

"There's no large runway for planes to make a decent landing on."

"Our old air field, which used to run from the river all the way to don Mamerto's house, was much better than the piece of shit airstrip there now."

"On the old field, although unpaved, Douglas aircraft, B-18s, Avros, big planes, used to land."

"Just small planes now."

"A piece of pockmarked landing strip they left us."

"They built the marketplace, the library, the radio station, a few ARIC warehouses, and they let everything go to waste."

"As if there were no space."

"Now the Army can't arrive either by plane or by land."

"The highway reached us 100 years after don Juan Ballinas asked for it."

And me, I listen to my father expound, and I write as if he were dictating to me.

But this armed movement is, say what you will, college-student ideology.

And, according to my reading of Gabriel Zaid, I doubt the college kids want the peasants to leave the field to become... college kids.[77]

And undergraduates from the big city must now be celebrating the violence on the outskirts of Coyoacán, in the cafeterias and in the lecture halls.

And many intellectuals must be dusting off their bellicose dreams, ready to hang, over the Che Guevara poster,[78] full of cobwebs, these new versions of heroes with boots on.

One thuggish speech and the entire leper colony was bid come forth, loosed and let go.

And one is left filled with doubt, without getting carried away, with no desire to applaud either the vulture, or the fly, or the dog, or the guerrilla willing to sacrifice 150,000 lives if necessary.

And my father justifies the uprising.

And my mother radically disapproves of it.

And I'm this bundle of misgivings with one sole conviction: the new tyranny is always nesting in the depths of a warrior's soul.

And that's what I'm writing when my cousin Mario arrives.

Tells us about a schoolteacher who lives near his house: is from Taniperla, a collective settlement in the jungle.

His mom came to spend Christmas and New Year's with him, here.

They live in a wooden house.

The schoolteacher's young son wanted to look out the window, one day during the shootout.

A little boy.

His grandmother came over to pull him away.

Those were moments of heavy combat.

A bullet penetrated through the wood.

Grazed the back of the child's neck and hit the woman. She's dead.

Her name was Basilia.

Mario and Ovidio helped bury her.

Have been active helping neighbors who suffered damages.

Saw the guerrillas escaping along the creek because their house is right next to it.

Saw many wounded.

"That female captain, the squad leader or whatever she was, passed by shouting: 'Shoot, cowards, shoot! Fire! Don't let them close in!' But she was already wounded."

And Mario continues:

"The shootout was whizzing around our heads as we were making a fire for tortillas. Right now all's clear.

"People are now cleaning their houses and their patios. I began gathering shell casings. I have all sizes, from .22 all the way up to some that seem like small drinking glasses. I think they were from a bazooka or something like that. One day the soldiers detained Ovidio and me. We'd gone out into street. We told them that we lived right here, a block away, and they let us go. 'You have ten seconds to get home, after that we're gonna start shooting. Jeez Louise! We arrived in five seconds flat!"

Yesterday we saw Ruben in the marketplace. He's another of my cousins, the brother of these youngsters.

Ruben got married two weeks ago.

So, since yesterday we know nothing happened to them.

There're no casualties in the family.

Neither there nor here.

Yet.

12:45 We've heard nothing about my brother Rodulfo.

Pillita and I were going to stop by yesterday, on the way back from the cemetery, but the sepulchral silence in the streets prevented us.

We've decided to go right now to take them something my mother prepared for them to eat.

The neighborhood is calm.

Lots of people at their house doors.

We greet all our acquaintances.

Ask around.

Everything's OK.

Comes from the highway a Red Cross ambulance.

A military plane is flying overhead.

Just as we're arriving at my brother's house we see them coming, Conchita and him.

They were going home.

We delivered the package.

We go back together, the four of us.

13:00 We're about to go in when a press vehicle stops in front of us.

A red Volkswagen.

"Efraín!" they shout.

We're thinking it's Enrique Aguilar, who has a car just like it.

We come closer.

See the *Macropolis* logo.

It's Alejandro Toledo and Marco Vargas, from *Macropolis*, and Gustavo Armenta and Jean Sidenar, from *Cambio 7*.

Mention to us that they came by way of Tenejapa.

A large convoy of reporters was coming, but only those arrived.

They ask what I'm doing here.

I tell them I'm staying here at my parents' house, that I've been here since December 20th.

"We have to interview you," says Alejandro.

But first they'll tour the town.

They'll come back later.

13:16 The swarm of vultures has migrated down a bit, more toward the river, maybe further away.

I keep thinking about the dead bodies in the mountains.

14:47 Flor Domínguez informs us that the phone lines are back up.

We try calling Mexico City, but the calls aren't going through.

The line gets crossed with that of my cousin Lety, who's trying to call Córdoba.

We dial Dora's number: call goes through after several attempts.

Then nothing.

Busy signal.

16:40 The reporters left 10 minutes ago.

I read and commented on, skipping around, my diary entries from the first three days.

They recorded.

They must get to San Cristóbal and leave here soon.

Pilla reminds them there's a virtual curfew starting at 5 p.m.

17:00 Loud noise of bull horns proclaiming.

It's the Mayor, who atop an Army truck, proclaims that now life can now go back to normal, that now people can come out into the streets.

These are the phrases that are repeated: "Thanks to our glorious Mexican army, Ocosingo has been rescued. Thanks to our glorious army, everything has returned to normal. We can now move about freely. Thanks to the Mexican Army, everything will be the same again."

But well all know that nothing will ever be the same again.

People comment, walk away.

There are lots of them across from the burned town hall, as far as my wife and I have gone down.

17:30 Despite the saddening atmosphere that the burned building causes, people's eyes glisten distinctly.

The soldiers ask me for identification before entering the park.

Just me.

People chat with the soldiers, humble people, appreciative.

It surprised me a while ago to see how people were coming outdoors to shout hurrays for the Army, to applaud the soldiers.

It's strange to see.

The tough soldiers try to maintain their expressionless faces but a smile betrays them.

There are youngsters, predominantly, among the troops.

Kids just over 18.

People form little groups, greet each other, chat.

They begin sweeping the streets.

Strange calm protected by the Army.

The sky continues exquisitely blue and all swallows of the valley seem to organize their fluttering underneath the transparency.

I sit on a bench, I watch, I write.

What poetic truth is there in all of this?

One: the monster never emerges by accident.

It's always a call to attention from the Great Mother, to point out to us that we've violated basic poetic principles.

And in Chiapas it's so obvious.

Attacks upon the earth, upon the rivers, upon the jungle.

It's true that in these fertile valleys people don't die of hunger: the poorest person sows a cornfield and a beanfield, on his own land or on another's.

And sows plantain, keeps beehives and in any old hovel, there are pigs, turkeys, hens.

But there's racial hatred.

But there's caste war.

And there are corrupt judges, corrupt officials, corrupt teachers.

And exploitative business types with debased moral values.

And hatred between inhabitants of Ocosingo and Oxchuc.

And slow infiltration by the saviors of souls.

And gamesmanship.

And skullduggery.

And, mixed with all that, a surprising capacity for work.

In the field hand: the farmer and the cattle breeder.

These men with sun burnt skin and rough hands who rise at dawn and are at their ranches by five in order to be back in town at six, delivering milk that will be drunk or will be turned into cheese, into cream, into butter.

These cowboys who now drive pick-up trucks.

These men of bad taste who produce that which we shall eat in the big cities.

These men and women couldn't study because they had to tend their ranches.

These to whom reality is suddenly become so incomprehensible.

And Ocosingo can never be the same as before.

Because for some time to come the hatred will mount.

And the wounds won't heal easily.

And "monsters of the good" will continue arriving in the valley.[79]

And while this passes, hastily, through my head, the valley herons flutter off to their magnificent tree.

The sun now sets behind the immense Chacashib mountain range, amid red resplendences.

Like an oriental king, the sun expires.80

18:32 We encounter Moisés Trujillo, the man whose house the unexploded grenade fell into.

Today Judicial Federal Policemen removed it.

"'Kick it away, like a ball,' the son of bitches were telling me." "Ah, fuck; if you guys who are the experts don't dare do it."

We also greet schoolteacher Jorge Meza, who tells us that on the 30th and 31st, his surprised wife told him: "Hey, Jorge, you shoulda seen how the red bandanas are selling! They gonna use 'em for the school dance or what? Imagine our surprise when we saw what they wanted them for, look!—and raises his extended hand, in a rapid gesture, up to his nose— What a bunch a bastards!"

And the schoolteacher continues:

"Me, sure I was pissed with everyone who was stealing. You'll forgive me, but I even got to insulting those were passing by carrying their things. Some women from over there, here they came struggling with packages of toilet paper. Packages bigger than they were! They just passed by and I said right out loud to my wife: 'and these broads, who were wiping their asses with corn cobs up until yesterday, what do they want that for'?"

Images from the park: two girls see each other, run towards each other, hug, kiss, want to speak, cry and laugh all at once. They thank God.

Some girls and guys have their pictures taken with the soldiers.

"Get the truck in the shot," a gentleman orders.

We meet up with Domingo, a young Tzeltal who lives near El Chorro.

Greet each other with joy.

—Good thing God didn't want us die in war, yes indeedy!, he says laughing, in his pidgin Spanish. Then asks: They killt that guy Palatsá, that true?

—Who?

—That guy Jorge Palatsá, pot-bellied like this, big dark-skinned guy.

—I don't think so, Domingo—I respond—we'd have known about it already.

—But people was sayin' they killt that don Pepe Barragán too, and don Alí, and that don Chuchín Rovelo, that they even cut his nuts off with a machete.

And he was laughing hard, Domingo, asking those questions.

—They's also sayin' they killt don Roch.
—Well, there's the corpse—I tell him.
He goes back where I indicate: there's Rodolfo Ruiz, with Lucy, his wife, and Jorge López, the presumed deceased fat guy: they're chatting on the sidewalk of their house.

—People tellin' lies... yessiree Bob!—concludes good ole Domingo, dying with laughter.

There was a group opposite Gardenia Pharmacy.
Someone, from over in the park, comments: "They looked like fresh-bought chickens in a new coop, those rich people."[81]
Another one, half-nostalgic and half pitiable: "Ooh now, the Citizens' Defense Committee didn't do a damn thing."
"Well, no, we were all scared," they respond.
We go down to the church: people are going in, crying, making the sign of the cross.
Praising God.
Some right out loud.
Priests greet people at the entrance.
Shake hands, speak to everyone.
Some leave suddenly, after crossing themselves, right there at the entrance.
Others get as far as the Nativity, opposite the great altar.
Sit down on the cedar pews.
Pray.

"Lotta good the fucking priests did," says a man on the convent sidewalk.

Is there really racism in town?
Certainly.
"Injun!" "Injun!" "Injun!"
The word cleaves the air with the reverberant effect of a machete blow on a heart of oak.

"No-good Indian," "miserable Indian," "you must a been a Indian," "Indian sonofabitch," "Indian in disguise," "black Indian," "you eat like a Indian," "you ride like a Indian," "you look like a Indian," "Indians are nasty and filthy," "they're thieves," "all Indian offspring look alike."

Or the reaction formation:[82] "little Indians," "pure-souled indians," "noble Idians," "essentially good Indians," "little Indians who must be helped," "exploited Indians," "Indians enslaved on the farms," "poor little Indians," "Indians who won't be able to do anything if enlightened Ladinos don't come put *learning in their eyes, maize in their mouths, bibles in their pockets, guns in their hands.*

And I cannot be at peace: I think about that chilling thesis that views war as a natural mechanism for regulating overpopulation; or I think about the human condition: a forcemeat of angel and demon, as in Parra's verse.[83]

We go back home beneath the lukewarm night.

7 JANUARY [84]

8:22 My sister Mapi leaves with her family: Luis, her husband; Rosario, Domingo, Karen and Ámbar, their children.

They leave for Palenque, taking advantage of the Red Cross bridge.

A long caravan forms at the town exit: those who came to spend the holidays with their parents are leaving.

There's lots of crying at the family farewells.

9:21 A bang is heard toward the southwest.

9:56 Bang toward the northeast.

No one says so but we're all worried: that way lies the road to Palenque.

10:32 I write half-heartedly.

Won't let this sorrow creep in.

Am worried about my children, the family members who just left, the reporters from yesterday.

The thuds have been heard sporadically.

If I want to be useful around the house this pain has to be managed, this fatigue, this boredom.

Lots of dump trucks begin collecting garbage from town.

Lots of movement is seen in the streets.

Vehicular traffic begins circulating.

Some people already left for their ranches, especially the ones over here from the Jataté.

There's an army roadblock at Pequeñeces.

Water started running out again.

Dora and Génner went back to their house in Barrio Magisterial.

Found that all was well, although people hadn't gotten up the courage to go out.

I'm going to plant a yellow sapote seed, a delicious
tropical fruit, yellow-orange in color, with a taste somewhere
in between the sapodilla fruit and the mammy apple.[85]

Action to face down depression.

The busy bee has no time for sorrow.[86]

12:24 "When the guerrillas let the prisoners out, they were
gonna string up the guy who was carrying the keys. He handed
them over. All the prisoners left with the guerrillas, including
the gringo accused of killing a little 12-year-old girl from the
Lacandon jungle."

That's what Juan, a man who keeps a corn field on the
little ranch, a plot of land across from my house in El Chorro,
tells us.

Juan lives very nearby.

My father lets him keep a cornfield on the land where he
keeps 12 beehives in addition.

He pays nothing in return, but does deeds like what he
did today: brought my mother a big pouch full of green beans.

"Here, I brought you this little gift, doña Celinita... for
these days of such great misery."

A woman comes by to sell pork.

"I slaughtered two and I'm almost out already."

18:00 The day dragged slow.

I devoted myself to taking out coffee, to shucking green
beans with the children, to planting seeds.

Today we ate another gigantic rooster from the orchard.

All day planes and helicopters of various sizes and shapes
arrived.

Were bringing people pantry items.

Have been landing on high school fields and on the now
repaired airstrip.

Very long lines of women awaiting pantry items formed.

Comment at the park: "The women who were looting in
the stores were the first ones asking for pantry items. People
have no shame!"

Lots of people came for doctor's visits.

At about 5 o'clock I bathed.

Went upstairs to read.

That I do.

§

19:30 The electricity goes out.

If it doesn't come back on in five minutes the town will spend another restless night.

This morning we were commenting on that at the corner: anxiety increases in darkness, everybody's afraid the town will be invaded.

"For some reason they're cutting off the electricity."

"And since the guerrillas threatened that if they came back now it would be to kill for sure."

19:50 Shelling toward the northeast.

Also in the southwest.

The loud noise keeps on, more or less continuous.

Lasts a long time: more than 20 minutes.

Once again widespread fear.

I go get my uncle Rodrigo, in his room, on the other side of the upper patio.

We place chairs in my parents' room.

We're all here.

20:12 You can hear the clock's tick-tock amid the silence.

Our silence.

In the adjoining room, my sisters, nieces and nephews.

Edgar and Génner must be there.

One shot from a small pistol is heard near the school.

21:23 Relaxed conversation in the dark.

Thuds to the northeast.

Another one, as I'm making this entry.

We've had coffee and we each decide to go to our room.

21:30 More thuds.

We've moved our bed to a sort of niche, in the bedroom Mapi and her family were occupying.

A sort of niche, I meant, with secure walls, with no large window nearby, where a very large closet will be built.

I write by the light of a small candle.

Nearby thuds.

23:00 Periods of sweet dreams in the midst of fear.

Through the window I see the sky marvelously clear.

I go out in total darkness.

The sky gives off a very peaceful light.

Toward all four points of the compass stars shine.

Magically clear sky.

The vault of heaven deserving of its name.

Isolated shots are heard, but that doesn't matter underneath this sky.

I invite my wife.

We take out a mat, blankets, pillows.

And lie down on the terrace floor to contemplate the sky at length.

8 JANUARY[87]

7:30 A plane sounds overhead.

07:45 Another plane, or the same one on its way back.
I see soldiers in the school buildings and town hall, at the pharmacy and the hotels.

Carmelino's nervous: they've warned him that "there're 500 Indians on the outskirts of town."
That they're holing up at small ranches beyond the Jataté.
"Working so hard all your life just so these sons of bitches can come steal what didn't cost them a thing," says, at the store, a young man whom I don't know.
It's been 32 years since I left Ocosingo, first for San Cristóbal and then for the monstrous city. It's changed so much: of the small populated area of 3,000 inhabitants, of cobble-stone streets, orchards and coffee plantations, and streets criss-crossed by horses skillfully ridden by able cowboys, not even the memory remains. There was no highway and all dealings with the outside world used to be done via small planes. Progress came and came at a cost. Uglified the architecture, chopped down the orchards, paved the streets over and filled them with noise and filth. I'm writing this because there're so many people I no longer recognize.
The violent rumble of the planes has kept us all whispering, tip-toeing around, indoors.
The furious purr stitches clouds together with an invisible thread.
At this hour, in Mexico City, my children must be in class, listening to university harangues in favor of the armed rebels.

08:57 We finished a barricade with cement blocks, to protect a window of my parents' room.

Génner, Edgar, uncle Rodrigo, Pillita and I did it, transporting blocks barehanded or with uncle Mario's dolly.

We managed to move half a ton.

It was cloudy at first light.

It drizzled before dawn, amidst a hair-raising wind.

The birds of paradise, which we planted a year ago, arise in all their radiant splendor.

I gaze at the Surinam cherries and the tulips, the roses and the bougainvillea, brilliantined by the drizzle.

I think about my children again: according to our plans, today we were supposed to be on our way back.

I want to be in Mexico City, but if I were there I'd want to be here.

People go around with their white flags beneath the drizzle.

Edgar sees patients.

"The Indians are holing up on the ranches out past Guadalupe, to look for arms, small rifles and pistols. But also to steal beans, corn, sugar, salt. They're going around saying that now they're definitely gonna come kill everyone in town."

This I hear in the doctor's office, in whose doorway I've come to sit and write, while I look out at the street.

09:55 A employee from town hall comes looking for Adán Sánchez, my neighbor and godson's father, who lives across the way and is the municipality's leading town councilor.

The boy says the neighboring communities are peaceful: that there's nothing going on in Rancho Mateo, nor in Campet, nor in Suschilá.

That there's nothing to fear.

10:00 Alfonso Victoria tells the story, in the waiting room of the doctor's office: "Nine shots entered my room. One was left like this, all twisted, a piece of lead. Thing is, I live near Balthazar Ruiz, who's got a really big place, with lots of trees. There were lots of Indians holed up there. It had our asses like this: contracting and expanding. We were scared shitless. It was rough. When the 15 helicopters passed by, all the guerrillas holed up there were shooting."

10:15 Jesús, Celia's son-in-law who lives up the street, stops by.

He went all the way to the roadblock and they told him the Red Cross is still helping those who want to leave.

They have two buses and people can also leave in their own vehicles.

He and his whole family are thinking of leaving: his mother-in-law, his sister-in-law, everybody.

"Thing is, we're really worried about the children. They cry a lot. They're scared. If you didn't have kids, you'd go out and kill them or whatever, but with little ones..."

Carmelino's also thinking about leaving, "if he gets some gas."

Adán tells about a lady whom they pierced through the chest with a bullet: "Titty swollen out to here... but she's still alive, she didn't die."

He also gives us the heads up that Eleuterio's son passed by, saying "don't get too comfortable, because 500 men are coming ready to finish off the town."

I ask my sister who's the oft-mentioned Eleuterio: "An old man who lives up here. Just got out of jail. Has trucks and seems to be making trips to the jungle."

11:07 There've been no impacts all morning.
Or have there?

11:21 I cut up some cartons and place them in the windows of my parents' room.

This will allow for turning on the light without feeling anxiety by night.

We're still without electricity, but the water's running.

11:35 Carmelino's leaving.

He refused to stop to do any more business.

"There's only a little liquor left now," he says.

"Brave as your father was and you so cowardly," Elva Ruiz tells him.

"Yeah. It's just that last night I was scared, plain and simple. You can't even sleep. I'm real nervous all day long," he responds.

"And Flor's really nervous, too," says Dora.

Carmelino's sure the two tons of dynamite that were stolen from Pemex are going to be used to blow up the town.

"And my house can't withstand not even two shells," he adds.

Pilla and Dora found a store where they're selling plantains.

11:49 I put flower pots on top of the barricade blocks.

The wind and drizzle grow stronger, and savage the cluster of palm trees that's grown on the west patio.

But there're lots of palm trees, royal and coyol, in nearby places.

At la Celia's house, at doña Leonor's house, at what was doña Leonides' house.

There're big avocado trees in ours and in the neighboring vegetable gardens.

All this adds to the sound of the wind in the foliage.

Music of the turbulent palms.

From San Cristóbal, at 7,283 feet above sea level, descends the mountain range towards the east.

Little by little, amidst hollows, hills and miniscule valleys.

Thick with conifers and checkered by cornfields and collectives, settlements and wilderness areas, the mountain range smoothes as it slides towards our warm valleys.

Hills, ocote pines, oaks, clouds and the Jataté itself, all come visit the valley.

The hills stop short, prudent, at La Ventana.

The audacious Jataté spills over in a torrent of foam: a violent explosion of whiteness that bursts into tempestuous cascades.

Soon it's pacified, and its green transparency is confined to the three valleys.

It then becomes the Lacantún River and much later, now joined with the Usumacinta, will discharge the greatest volume of water that any Mexican river spews out into the Gulf.

12:40—Why's it raining so hard, grandma?—quizzes Edgar, the littlest grandchild.

—It's the Cabañuelas, child.[88] Today is August. Yesterday the rains began, in July. Because of this lousy war, we haven't even paid attention to the Cabañuelas.

12:41 A caterpillar: a prodigy of hair and antennae, passes, extremely slow, by the low terrace wall.

Its multiple little feet move it along with a quickness, like chills running up and down the spine of shuddering itself.

It seems almost feathered.

An undiluted horror.

12:45 Mist has sepulchered the town.

You can see the church but absolutely nothing beyond.

The soldiers, on the school roof, stand guard beneath the drizzle.

12:50 The hog-butcher lady brings us the lard we ordered yesterday.

Today they didn't slaughter because "it's scary to go out selling. On account of last night."

13:00 Don Beto Ruiz recounts how "as the guerrillas were leaving, they came and killed two my little cows. Just for the hell of it. Since there was so much gunfire we couldn't make use of them, none of us. They rotted there... just vulture pickings."

13:07 Rich against poor, Indians against Ladinos, Catholics against Protestants, people from Ocosingo against people from Oxchuc.

And all possible combinations of those eight variables.

Plus the new variables within each category.

An example?

Here goes: Poor Indians against rich Indians.

Poor Ladinos against rich Ladinos.

Poor Oxchuc Indians against poor Ocosingo Ladinos.

Poor Protestant Indians against poor Catholic Indians.

Rich Protestants against rich Catholics.

Rich Catholics against poor Catholics.

Rich Samuelist Catholics against rich anti-Samuelist Catholics.

Rich pacifist Ladinos against poor Indians, politicized and aggressive.

Rich Ocosingo Ladinos, aggressive, Catholic, conservative, anti-Samuelist, against...

Everyone at war with everyone, in this area of the world that burns quietly beneath the drizzle.

13:15 The street, without the store and its customers, looks lonelier.

My father says that "Carmelino left because his store's called 'El Cubanito.' So, they might ask him to support the cause."

We chuckle.

13:20 Domingo and Martín, father and son, Tzeltals, come to the house.

Bring two bunches of bananas.

These displays, which so move my wife, seem absolutely natural to me.

I've seen them throughout my life.

Displays of gratitude that speak of respect and reciprocity.

Clearly, in time of war the spotlight shines brighter on gestures like this.

14:02 It's Saturday.

Finally, after so long, we heard a little marimba on the radio.

Laughter, like on the program *La Tremenda Corte*.[89]

Alarming news: 400 guerrillas try to take over the San Cristóbal microwave station.

A bomb at University Plaza.

Another in Acapulco.

Alarm because of another explosive device at the Legislative Palace in Mexico City.

14:34 The drizzle hasn't stopped all morning.

14:36 Lety calls, my cousin: saying Carmelita Villafuerte heard the news on the radio that yesterday's caravan arrived safely in Tuxtla and San Cristóbal.

My sister and her family, my aunt and her family, my cousin Toño and his family, they arrived without incident.

19:32 Last night we were worried that the light from the windows could be seen.

In the morning I put cardboard between the glass and the curtains.

It was perfect: now we can light candles and kerosene lamps calmly.

Dora made some delicious bread that we had with recently ground coffee at the candle-lit table.

The afternoon went by without major incident.

Many townspeople left.

It's inevitable, they'll continue leaving.

Today, with the necessary precautions, the barricade, orderliness, we went to bed with greater calm.

The drizzle didn't stop all day.

Was increasing at times.

I think about those boys, the rebels in arms.

Imagine them underneath the drizzle during these days of suffering.

Think about the people from the ranches sleeping out in the bush, also underneath the drizzle and wind, fleeing from the rebels.

Imagine them asking the children not to make noise because the guerrillas might discover them, because they might kill them.

And also think about the young soldiers standing guard at the roadblocks.

With their eyes peeled for every silhouette, for every shadow.

With their ears peeled for each nocturnal noise, for each animal cry, for each screech owl, for each branch that breaks.

Behind any given tree death may lie in wait.

9 JANUARY[90]

9:12 Day breaks cloudy but without drizzle.

There're instructions to place a white flag on houses because the Army will pass by pointing out empty houses.

Planes have been flying overhead since 7:30 a.m.

The soldiers are still in place.

A dead dog appeared on the sidewalk.

How will it be, the country these men in arms dream of?

Is it easier organizing in order to kill than it is to produce?

Hasn't there been enough bloodshed?

Were not better winds blowing, really, even in these forgotten lands?

Isn't enough blood spilled in Guatemala, in El Salvador, in Cuba, in Nicaragua?

More blood to fertilize the soil of Utopia?

And all for what?

I hear, on the radio, about a government commission consisting of people from Chiapas: Andrés Fábregas[91], Eduardo Robledo[92] and Eraclio Zepeda.[93]

A peace commission.

Peace: you never know just how good you got it till you ain't got it no more.

I overhear these words: "they were dragging the dead away with a lasso to burn them. They made all onlookers at the marketplace pull the dead body away. They were already hauling Doctor Talango off to the fire too, but some of don Enrique's workers recognized him."

There're no classes, there's no electricity, there's no telephone.

Rumor's been spreading around that mass will be said at twelve o'clock.

But they won't chime church bells so people won't get frightened.

Many people left: almost all the schoolteachers.

And my father says: "What kind of teachers can they be? What education are they giving the children? What civics lessons?"

13:29 We return from mass: there were about 150 people despite the fact that they didn't ring church bells.

There'll be another mass at four in the afternoon.

Father Pablo Iribarren's message revolved around baptism.

The meaning of baptism and this baptism by blood that bathed us in reality.

He asks that this baptism change our vision and better the people of Chiapas, improve Mexico, better humanity.

Asked that a prayer be said for the dead of the town, of the armed faction, of the Mexican Army.

Begs God's forgiveness for us all.

Tears in the eyes of many women.

Said that, according to the latest news, the EZLN had agreed to a dialogue.

Arriving at the exit door we saw a group of judicial federal police escorting Geno López, the Mayor's brother.

Geno says hello to me and afterwards they go in.

Two stand guard at the door.

Black jackets with big white letters: JFP.

Sub-machine guns, dark glasses, menacing physiques.

Black jackets on Zapatistas and Judicial Federals.

And even though it's broad daylight, I think about Federico García Lorca's masterly verse: "Civil Guardsmen hunchbacked and nocturnal."[94]

The cold continues but the lights come back on.

A soldier informs us that 1,200 cavalry entered through the jungle, by way of Chancalá, and that they'll reach the border.

That it was indeed true about the skirmish at La Cumbre.

That 14 guerrillas died there.

"One bastard somewhere around ETA, he sure put up a fight. He was a very good shot. It took us a long time to finish him off. About 13 or 14 he was, the bastard."

16:45 My wife goes to get cloves and black pepper at aunt Flor's house.

She'll fix me some tea for my cold.

On her way back she meets up with Arístides.

At that moment a cowboy from the San Antonio ranch arrives, with a horse and a mule.

Says that people from "down yonder," from Las Tazas, are ganging up and are daily killing one "rich people's" cow.

"If I didn't come back, they were gonna kill me, too. Better I came back. What's the point of me tending the cows if they're killing them anyway?"

Adán Sánchez reports that they detained Eleuterio and let him go after questioning.

20:22 Oswaldo and Paca come upstairs to report that at 22:00 hours there'll be a message about Chiapas current events, on channel 2.

We're still cut off from the outside world.

Tomorrow my psychotherapy practice was supposed to be starting.

I was supposed to collect my children's survivor's pension on the 5th.

The probate hearing was scheduled around that date.

What a pain.

I want to leave and want to stay.

10 JANUARY[95]

Another resplendent day.

Scant white clouds to the north, the rest is blue sky.

The eastern mountain range, a first body of intense greenery and a second mass of blue, is outlined with marvelous clarity.

Everything seems so peaceful.

But the superlatively blue sky was now knifed by helicopters and planes.

11:30   Soldiers are running along the school roof.

As if they'd received an alert.

11:35   Gunshots on the corner where the tortilla shop is.

Screaming and shouting.

Movement of soldiers in the street.

We run to close the entry gate and the doors.

My sister Dora's at Lety's house.

Military planes fly overhead.

Rumor's spreading: a guerrilla came to buy tortillas.

He's one of the ones left trapped in town, "at his brother-in-law's house."

His squad held a family hostage.

Someone from that family recognized him and tipped off the Army.

The soldiers came, fired into the air, already detained him.

It never ceases to amaze, people's gratitude toward the soldiers: they applaud them, shout cheers at them, bring them food, give them coffee.

"Yesterday people from Barrio Guadalupe brought them food. And the soldiers made them eat first. To make sure the food wasn't poisoned."

What must the ranches "down yonder" be like?

Nuevo México, Tijuana, Dolores, El Recreo, El Paraíso, San Antonio, San Lorenzo, Santa Rita, Ashín, Tecojá, El Real, the old ranches, the old means of field production, and the relentless onslaught of time that has blighted them in recent years.

Don José Cruz, owner of Toniná, remembering times past, reports: "It was something to see how they used to live at San José, for example. From far away you'd recognize Indians from San José, just by the whiteness of their clothes. They were people who'd learned how to work. They used to make their own blankets on their own looms. They planted the best cornfields, the best beanfields. They knew how to make pouches, nets, hats, clay pots, textiles, tostadas, you could buy everything there. They used to raise tobacco and made puro cigars; what puros, sir! The big house, a really big house with support beams and cedar columns, ceilings made of fine wood, wooden floors too. And the corral: a huge corral of pure stone. And the carved doors, the windows likewise, all surrounded by corridors with benches. Not to mention the furniture and fixtures. How gorgeous. Such refinement. But they were taking it all away from poor don Mario. Till he died of rage."

The industry of farm estates which the Dominicans built in these valleys more than four centuries ago.

They established those means of farm production and built that beautiful house, as they did all the big homesteads.

The Reform grabbed those properties from the clergy and divided them up among the liberal ranchers: the homesteaders.[96]

San José came to be called San José la Reforma.

Beginning with Cárdenas' land reform movements, the enormous spread of the farm estates was dwindling down to nothing, save for nuclei of population increasingly abundant, larger, more miserable, less productive, more in need of government assistance.[97]

Concludes don José Cruz: "Now you'll see what's left of San José. You'll find only misery. The Indians finished off everything. But of course, they're a bunch of bums. And even more so without a boss."

I listen to the old rancher's reasoning: a way of thinking that 50 years haven't ended up sweeping away, but whose ashes the Zapatista winds will surely scatter.

And I'm unsure whether for better or for worse.

What's certain is that it's inevitable.

12:46 I'm writing on the terrace, next to the clay pots from Amatenango, huge ones, which we bought a year ago December.

The sun burns despite the fact that the sky's been clouding over in the east.

A Great Kiskadee, very large, is eating medlar tree fruit in the foliage.

14:45 Enter an Army convoy, which seems to be coming from San Cristóbal.

Trucks jam-packed with soldiers, jeeps, clothing trucks, tanks, tanker trucks, armored personnel vehicles, an ambulance.

Twenty, twenty-five, thirty units?

"This only used to be seen in September 16 parades, on television."[98]

"With that weaponry they're gonna kill off everything, down to the last little jungle bunny."

And one humble woman, an old lady almost, who's heard talk of "goat horns,"[99] makes this comment of literal-mindedness: "So many weapons! How were the poor little Indians going to handle the soldiers? Although they tricked them. They say that to send them off to fight they gave them only wooden rifles and some goat *horns*, like knives maybe."

In the sky, the C-130 Hercules planes seem like dirigibles.

I go down to the town center to try and get a roll of film.

See the gigantic line from the Army food pantries.

18:00 Afternoon passes.

Arístides sends a little bread.

A bit of warm bread in a war situation.

Thanks!

Helicopters and planes brought the pantry items: the aerial flotillas have been landing all day.

A young man from the National Human Rights Commission[100] passes by requesting reports of people who have been disappeared or of ill treatment on the Army's part.

Pilla and I go buy a new coffee mill.

The guy from Human Rights is also requesting "messages for those who may have family in San Cristóbal" and is giving reports about the imminent reinstallation of telephone communications.

Comments overheard throughout the day:

Alfredo Díaz: "I cursed out the motherfuckers who left. I didn't even leave town, I who was Mayor, I whom they said stole, who was even put in jail for a few days. Our family, our house, our children are still here."

"They detained two of Eleuterio's sons."

One woman, in the pantry line: "And that lousy, bald-headed, fat-ass bitch, she still has the nerve to come asking for pantry items, after all the stuff she stole at the ISSSTE store."

An elementary school teacher: "Those leaders were here yesterday, Hernández and Jacobo. Who knows how they got in. Those guys are mixed up in this mess."

"The ones from the Coelhá collective are very involved; all of them I think."

"Uhm... about 20 years ago now they were going around Guanal training." A schoolteacher whose community was affected in that area: "During the night, the community remained siiilent. The next day they all looked very tired. At night only women and little kids would stay behind."

"They holed up at El Porvenir, they're holing up at the ranches down yonder to look for small arms, for hunting, and

sometimes they destroy everything or take beans and corn."
"So many people suffering so much, for what?"

"These ideas of the bishop's! He wants everybody to be doctors or engineers. Well, who's gonna work the land, then? And the cattle? Indians don't like to tend livestock. They're scared of cows."

"Morons, lazy bums! They say they did it because under socialism no one will carry firewood anymore!"

"They say if we leave town they won't let us back in for six months."

22:00   We hear on the radio that Patrocinio resigned. That President Salinas has named Manuel Camacho Solís as national peace commissioner.

II JANUARY¹⁰¹

Superlatively sunny day, blue, with the skirt of mist trailing the river's course: that dense swath that dissolves in air, without anyone noticing, at around nine in the morning, at the latest.

It's *8:52*.

I'll devote myself to observing that gradual disappearance.

Afternoon.
Once again the light I miss so much returns.
The light for which I return.
The gentle light of gold upon blue and green.
The gentle winged light on wingless hills.
Celestial breath.
Celestial air.
Luminous greenness.
Golden swaths above white clouds.
Evening aroma wafting from the humid garden.
For this light I have returned without realizing it.
This is what I've been searching for since the day I left.
God exists in each leaf, in each gentle gust of fresh scent.
The scent of night jasmine fills me with an inward splendor.
My valley returns little by little to peace.
When we men disappear, those sightless lights shall remain over the valley.
The afternoon warblings are muffled now; some long, sweet; others short and sharp, trilling in the darkness.
The valley.
Our valley.
The land where we were born and which we learned to love unwittingly; even in spite of ourselves, perhaps because of this light.
Just because of that light that's gone away above.

Black town.

Hills.

The two lines of hills (those of nearby green and those of faraway blue) muddled suddenly in a mass of blue that borders upon black.

Then the sky of light sky blue: the delicate blue where, pulsating, the first star begins to shine.

In the morning we went to the cabin to plant two pacaya palms and one night jasmine shrub.

We stopped by my brother Rodulfo's house for a handsaw.

We needed it to cut an oak support beam where we'd put the mill base.

We went along the river.

Along the old path where I still encounter the town in which I lived.

My old town.

We saw the ceiba tree belonging to the little old house on the small ranch.

Saw the new bamboo flourishing vigorously.

Guadalupe went down with Rodulfo to harvest allspice.

There were no more seeds.

Each year it's produced by the bushel and most of it's wasted.

Nobody harvests it although my mother says people are stealing it.

My parents planted each and every tree of that vegetable garden.

That's why my mother's saddened that those "who sow nothing" should steal the fruits.

We were about to go up to our Casa de la Luna, just past the highway, when Génner arrived.

Informed me that Eraclio ("Laco") Zepeda had arrived in town and wanted to see me.

A messenger from the Mayor's office arrived, and we received a telephone call from Manuel, Laco's brother.

They were only going to be in town an hour.

We had 20 minutes left.

Went down.

Found Manuel.

Afterwards Eraclio, Fábregas, Robledo Rincón arrived: the peace commission.

Provide encouraging information.

They're excited.

Tomorrow they'll meet with representatives of 70,000 peasant farmers who are against the armed struggle.

They already negotiated the journalists' entrance with the Army.

Indeed: the journalists arrived minutes later in three helicopters.

In the park, extremely long line of people awaiting food relief.

Some of them had been waiting four or five hours, continued on there, disciplined, stoic.

"It's no longer like before when even in this town's humblest home there was food to eat."

"At least beans, corn, vegetables, plantains."

Everything changed, for the worse, with progress.

So says my *innermost reactionary sadness*.[102]

So I was thinking while I watched the long line of women who, crowded in line, covered eight blocks or so.

I never saw so many women in town.

Laco appeared, his bulk as abundant as his soul, offering solidarity, support, help in leaving town.

We thanked him, but still decided not to leave.

They took pictures of us.

We went back home.

But first Pilla went into the church to get my mother a piece of Paschal candle.[103]

I stayed behind contemplating the town's large plaza covered in cement.

The old colonial fountain destroyed by a certain mayor who wanted to "renovate" it.

The beautiful colonnades, formerly white, now besmirched by commercial signs.

Miss Chayo Solórzano's lovely house, previously belonging to aunt Vidaura, which could have been a beautiful cultural center (a mini museum, a heritage house), and which has been miserably wasted and used for Judicial branch offices and before that as PRI offices.

The old exceedingly beautiful roofs that used to surround the colonial plaza now very much afflicted by the garish colors and extremely ugly "modern" pharmacy buildings.

My old plaza.

My old park full of ceiba trees, privet trees, flame trees.[104]

I didn't know the great ceiba tree John Lloyd Stephens admired in the mid 19th century.[105]

Nor did I know the privet trees of the 1920s.

But I did indeed know the great flame trees that used to set the day on fire with explosions of red and yellow, and would filter out the sun with delicate little green hands, as if sifting through it.

Green filigree in the foliage of the flame trees.

Another mayor ordered the flame trees cut down and planted Indian Laurel trees.

In a place of such varied flora were planted those cookie-cutter trees that homogenized the park like any other impersonal park in the republic.

Ah, mayors.

"An errant crowd, municipal and thick."[106]

Not a single ceiba tree remains in the public spaces.

There is not a single caoba tree in the public spaces.

There is not a single cedar tree in the public spaces.

The spiritual squalor of a town victimized by a progress in which seems to have married the worst taste of the businessmen, the cattlemen, the oil men, the powers that be, the dirty society of the unscrupulous and the petty and the rabble.

Well, people.

People, in short.

My people.

Evening:

Some ladies are buying clothing at Teté's Novelities, my sister's store. They recount: "The Indians took my husband's truck from him in Monte Líbano. Just like the others. They arrived on foot. They told the Mayor on the 29th, and the Mayor said we'll see what the Governor said. Who knows if the Mayor warned the Governor. They also told the Mayor to warn the townspeople, so people would know about it. The Mayor said no. So as not to cause panic. Us, we left, sure did. My child's godparents too."

A man from near Queshil: "The guerrillas took my boss's van from me. They destroyed the whole house. All the livestock they killed in a hail of gunfire. Nothing was left. They even burned the corral. Same thing happened in Saboquité."

Three cowboys brought about 400 head of cattle from various ranches "down yonder." "But guerrillas armed to the teeth caught up with us. They opened fire and made off with the cattle on the way back. A cowboy from San Lorenzo went with them. Turned traitor."

Says don José Trujillo Burguete, the former town blacksmith; used to make horseshoes, swivels, branding irons, hinges, door latches, nose leads, etc. With the arrival of progress his old trade was lost. Now he buys and slaughters lambs for barbecues. Comes to the house to buy lambs. I hear him chewing the fat with my father:

—Well, seems like everything's on the right track—my father says—between the Zapatistas and the government. Don Samuel Ruiz is going to be the go-between.

—Ah, shoot! It's gonna get woise! That bastard Samuel! I don't know why they don't just disappear him once and for all. He's done enough damage already!

So do passions run.

12 JANUARY[107]

Last night, I think I didn't note it here, the lights went out again.

We went another night without electricity.

We heard four shots or so, here and there, throughout the night.

Everybody now knows about the presidential "Cease Fire" decision.

Opinion either praises or condemns.

The Army forced the Zapatista troops to withdraw from the centers of population, and retreat toward the jungle.

And what it boils down to is this: dialogue or bloodshed.

And, judging by the tone of the war declaration, the rebels want bloodshed.

It's known that Camacho will arrive in Chiapas today.[108]

San Cristóbal radio reports that the Army has opened up the roads from San Cristóbal to Comitán, from San Cristóbal to Tuxtla, from San Cristóbal to Ocosingo: replenishments are on the way.

The day is clear, with clouds white upon the horizon.

Clouds cast shadows upon the hills.

Two planes fly over the populated area.

Today—they say—a Telmex work crew will come in to re-establish communications.

Conversations at the entry gate: a woman came to ask the soldiers' help because in Petultón they killed a family: a couple and their children.

Socorro Espinoza, widow of Alfonso Cruz, came to the medical office with Edgar.

She chats with my wife: "He came to see how the girls were holding up. 'What are you doing?', I said. 'They'll be alright, they're with their grandparents.' But he wanted to come. It was his destiny."

They say the rebels got into Jorge Ordóñez' ranch: robbed and killed animals.

That they're taking names of shopkeepers who are price gouging.

That yesterday they arrested some guerrillas at the Hotel Agua Azul, near the town center (everything's close by).

That a woman from El Salvador, married to the one of the guys from town, is missing.

That on the morning of day two they saw her "parading around brazenly in her Zapatista uniform."

That there are guerrillas in Chijtal cave.

"But this is going to go on and on, until the rich people are finished off."

10:16 A group of soldiers comes over.

Folks in our house are frightened.

I go out and look.

They're asking for "the owner of the store."

My sister's not here.

They want to buy socks!

I tell them they can come back later.

They go away.

Chabela Arcia tells us she informed the Ministry of Urban Development and the Environment about an enormous oak tree that had grown on her land, very near town, just past the highway. It was her pride and joy. An ancient and gigantic oak. "The Zapatistas chopped it up into firewood."

11:40 A little old lady Tzeltal, the likes of which you hardly see anymore (wearing a long, ribboned tzec skirt and white, Indian blouse) comes to tell Carmelino, on whose ranch she works, that they killed one of his cows.

"It's right there, that cow, tossed away. I came to ask what to do. They killed it just for fun."

We tell her Carmelino left, but that she should leave word at his brother Adán's house.

You can already tell by the traffic in the streets and on the highway.

12:10 A military plane flies over the town.

12:16 The first bus from San Cristóbal arrives: a Lacandonia line bus, blue and white.

Things are apparently returning to normal.

14:17 A health convoy arrives, with ambulances and medicines.

Electricity is restored.

15:00 Camacho's in Ocosingo.

He arrives at the park and greets the soldier who's passing out pantry items.

Those in front shout, "long live Salinas!" and "*¡viva México!*"

Those in back join the commotion of reporters carrying different kinds of cameras and wearing assorted quasi-military vests.

The powers that be, who'd been nowhere in sight until today, accompany the commissioner.

They've been present since the Chiapas commission came, yesterday.

"The ones who want to be in the driver's seat already know what they're gonna demand," says a woman in the pantry line.

The committee members go down toward the marketplace.

The death stench persists despite the lime and a certain minimal order.

Members of the committee enter and leave with impressive dispatch.

They go no farther than the hallway they entered by.

They hurry off fast amid the flurry of print journalists, the melee of broadcast journalists, and the parley of the committee.

It seemed as if everybody was waiting for their chance to demand, demand, demand.

We go back home.

Evening is coming on.

It's the last day of Cabañuelas.

"Tomorrow the lesser cabañuelas begin," my mother says.

I wear the stench of death all over me.

I think of the fallen youths.

I think of César Vallejo:

To armed suffering the poet offers salute.

Then I think about the wooden rifles, and remember Blake's verses:

Remove away that black'ning church
Remove away that marriage hearse,
Remove away that man of blood—
You'll quite remove the ancient curse.

17:00 What follows, as far as we can see, is pure politics.

"The science whose ultimate end should be the good of mankind," according to Aristotle.

Or "the conduct of public affairs for private advantage," according to Ambrose Bierce.

There'll be a bit of everything: shady dealings, public agendas, low and high politics.

The politicians love us so!

They're so concerned for our well being!

They're sooo little interested in personal gain!

Their selflessness is sooo great!

Ah, the talking heads of both the left and right.

Even so, they're preferable to the thugs of Hooded Despotism.

17:30 I close my diary.

You can already hear the troubled waters.

It's the last day of Cabañuelas.

Death is close at hand.

It may pass by without seeing us.

The wind swept the evening clean.
Left behind that sky of blue.
The imperturbable stars shall shine again, anon.

VOICES
FROM
CHIAPAS

They said this mystery never shall cease:
The priest promotes war, and the soldier peace.

—William Blake

ANDRÉS SÁNCHEZ

"Holy shit! I got outta that one alive! When those guys came in, I was still sloshed. They were 'bout to tell me to get up. 'There's a war on,' they were telling me. Say what?! I got pissed. I wanted to whip out my machete—good thing those guys didn't notice. I went out and looked: there was a lotta, a whole buncha guys. Later, they told me that people'd already opened up the stores. People were coming over there. Poor people, people who need it, were carrying off things to eat; but then they're poor, what can you do?, they need it; they were snatching whatever they could! So, sure, those who had they wits about 'em made out like a bandit; those that was a fool didn't grab nothin.' But everybody, even a lotta rich people, stole stuff. What a shame—shame, my ass! Maybe you and me have some shame, but a whole lotta people with money had no shame at all: a guy who works at Superior, three refrigerators, a stove and name-brand stuff he made off with! And that bastard has a shitload of houses all over town! Well, yeah... me, I didn't hardly grab nothin.' Only five sets of sandals; but because they were stolen God punished me: I couldn't make a single pair out of 'em. One in one color and one in another but all of 'em for the same foot! I had to throw it all away. Then, the shooting started, all day long, all night long, and all the next day, and both of us, me and my son-in-law, face down on the ground! The bullets were whizzing close by; and since my shack is made of wood I just held my hand here, on my forehead, 'cause if a bullet got me there, well, that'd be the end of me. Two days without eating and without being able to use the outhouse. Then the soldiers came, ransacked my place, and since I had my son-in-law's stuff there, they asked me why his things were there, and whose were they.

"'They belong to my son-in-law,' I told 'em, 'from his stand at the market.' 'Those guys didn't come in here?' 'I don't know; 'cause, me, I didn't go out once the shooting started; if those guys got in there, I didn't see it.' The soldiers asked me if they'd gotten into my little kitchen. But, God as my witness, I really didn't know! Sure enough, they holed up in another shack, my neighbors' place, because the owner wasn't home. Soldiers came and opened fire on 'em. Wood splinters were just flying everywhere! 'Fuck! I'm hit!' one soldier shouted. They brought him here, in the bathroom; the blood was still there, on some of my pipes. And then they shot into another small house and there was a woman drinking coffee with her grandson; the bullet grazed the back of the little one's head and entered the woman's chest. She just cried for about ten minutes and then she died. And now that it's all over, the soldiers said that they'd come to the war, that the guerrillas were the ones who started it, and that they were shooting at anything that moved. Nowadays, there's still a lotta soldiers around my house. They already told us you can't go out after six o'clock at night. 'If you want to live, stay inside. If you want to die, go on out,' that's what they told us. It's a messed up situation."

DON ENRIQUE

It's September 1994. I'm visiting don Enrique Solórzano at Palma Arecas, his house in Tuxtla Gutiérrez. He and his family have decided to live here after the war. Don Enrique is the son of don José Solórzano, nicknamed "the Mosquito" because of his shorter than average stature in this area of short people. Don José was a man of action who, despite having studied only until third grade, acquired considerable capital. He formed businesses: built the Pichucalco-Campeche railroad bed; took part in the refining of rubber; had a chiclería; from the age of 15 or 16 worked in the monterías of the Vega family, the Celorio family, etc. He was owner of one of the beautiful farm estates that the Dominican friars built during the colonial period: El Rosario, which measured nearly 12,000 acres, just like La Victoria and other ranches in the jungle. Don Enrique inherited El Rosario and further enriched his inheritance with farming and cattle ranching. In recent years his ranch La Palma, almost 1,000 acres, was invaded. They stole all the cattle ("we'll see if the government pays me back"). He managed to get a few livestock out but they burned down the house and ransacked it. They stole the horses and saddles. El Rosario and La Palma being invaded, he still keeps two small ranches: Bulushbac and Pasilhá, the latter measuring nearly 75 acres. Don Enrique suffered through the Zapatista attack at his Port Arturo house in Ocosingo. His house was robbed, he was forced to open his safe, the women in the family were expelled from the house; meanwhile he, his cousin and his sons-in-law were kidnapped, humiliated, submitted to mock firing squads and finally placed almost as a human barricade when the fighting broke out in the Ocosingo marketplace. We arrive, my wife and I, at his house in Tuxtla and a jovial and exceedingly amiable white-haired man greets us, accompanied by a lady of mature beauty, his wife, doña Olga. An 11-year-old boy comes to say hello. ("They kidnapped him too. His mom

cried and pleaded for them to let him go," they said in town.)
Don Enrique Solórzano narrates:

"Since the age of 18 I lived on ranches. On El Rosario I
lived and worked for 45 years. That's how my children were
raised, with hard work on ranches, producing maize, beans,
livestock. "For a long time we would hear stories. First was
the one about my goddaughter's father, Cardel. He lived
in Ocosingo, became my compadre, I was the godfather of
one of his daughters. One time he arrived with some men
who came looking for barbasco root, who were thinking of
extracting cortisone from the barbasco root. They holed
up in the jungle. They entered the farming collective of La
Victoria, on the left bank of the Jataté River, near Las Tazas.
The Mexican Army discovered them, detained them, found
weapons. They took Cardel away. He came back some time
later, this time with no teeth. They say one of his daughters is
in the jungle, with the Zapatistas... who knows. Once, a few
years ago, I saw my goddaughter somewhere around Cancún.
She recognized me, greeted me very warmly. One time she
asked me for a couple of bucks, and I sent them to her. When
I ran into her in Cancún I hadn't seen her since she was 5 or
6 years old.

"Well, living on the ranch, people were coming up to me
and saying: 'Boss, people are living over in the caves, there
are people, people who aren't from around here, hairy, bushy-
bearded, with fatigue caps, with weapons.'

"Those natural caves are enormous, have water. And I
knew that there were others in Las Tazas. "Well, when we
proved it, when I was sure, governor Patrocinio was notified
through the Cattle Breeders Association. Then we found out
that the Army entered the caves, some said they'd killed some
of them. An Indian compadre of mine came and told me there
were people with weapons, men and women. 'And how did you
find out?', I asked him. 'Because one of my sons is with them.
People bring them tostadas, beans, stuff. One day I went with
my shotgun to see what it was all about, pretended like I was
going hunting. And they stop me. There were people from
the ranch and other foreigners. What're you doing here, they

say to me. I'm following a deer, I work here, on the ranch, I'm hunting. Deer my ass! They grabbed me, tied me up, carried me off to the cave, held me. And suddenly I see my son. There he was. And my son didn't want to say anything. He was also asking me what I was doing there. Finally they let me go.'

"My compadre told me this during the Patrocinio era, like I said before. Then the indigenous people started with the threats. One day they flat out came to take over the town, town hall. We organized and drove them out with sticks and stones.

"On the night of December 31st people warned me, 'Here they come.' I had some weapons in the house, shotguns, rifles, pistols. Having been raised on ranches I've always liked hunting and had those weapons. A nephew, Army captain or major, married to Maro's daughter, now they're separated; he came to the house and told me that people with guns had arrived in town. This was about four or five in the afternoon. My son-in-law told me a while later that he would be spending New Year's Eve with his mother in Yajalón. I told him, 'be careful, we know an armed group came into town. We don't know where they are.'

"So, anyhow Talango went to Yajalón with his family and his holiday turkey. They came back a little while later. I don't know why they didn't just leave. We asked Ocosingo's mayor, who's my nephew: 'No, uncle, nothing's wrong.' We had dinner, perfectly calm. We spent New Year's Eve together and around five in the morning, a phone call. 'They're coming now.' I handed out the weapons. 'If they wanna come in here, they'll see what'll happen,' I was thinking. Then Luis Pascasio came and told me: 'Cousin, the Indians held me prisoner. They're coming this way. They already destroyed the guard tower.' At that moment I told my sons-in-law: 'Take it easy, we'll see.' That was when we saw they weren't Indians from around here: all of them armed with huge weapons, combat weapons, machine guns, things like that. 'Don't shoot,' I told my son's-in-law. I stowed the weapons. The rebels came, entered, collected the weapons, demanded my keys. 'For what,' I said. 'You're rich people. We're going to kill you.'

Then they aimed their weapons at my daughters. Made them take off their shoes. 'This is a revolution. President Salinas and the Governor are going to die. Long live the revolution.' They threatened me with the machine guns. 'Come on, open up the safe.' I had some new bills in there, I didn't even have it accurately counted. There were about twelve or fourteen thousand new pesos, which they'd paid me for corn. 'Open the safe.' 'I don't know how to open it.' 'Of course you do, open it!' We went back and forth like that for a little while. I'd lost all fear at this point. But my wife and daughters began pressuring me. 'Yeah, dad, open it for them.' And I opened it for them. At the moment they called the one who was aiming at me and he got distracted. I took the money and stuffed it in my pocket. When the other one came the safe was already open. I had a family souvenir, a gold-handle Smith & Wesson pistol with my initials in diamonds. They took it. Also a gold Rolex which I wore three times, if that many. My brother gave it to me as a present long ago and I had it tucked away for about 20 years because the watch band broke. It turned up among some old things when we moved house. I wanted them to fix it and they told me in Tuxtla that the repair would cost $4,000. They told me the watch was worth $20,000. The bastards took that, too. They took jewelry, small stuff, earrings, bracelets. And me with the money in my pocket. Me they didn't search. Everybody else, yes. My sons-in-law. I don't know whether out of pity or out of the respect I inspired in them but they didn't dare search me. 'Money!, Money!', is all they wanted. My wife insisted. My daughters, too. 'Give it to them already, papa.' I gave it to them. They took it. They told my wife and daughters to get out, that the house was no longer theirs, told them to fuck off. They were El Salvadorans, or Guatemalans. One knows how people from around here talk, whether Indians or Ladinos. One knows what the Altamirano, Comitán, San Cristóbal, Tuxtla, coastal, Oxchuc accent sounds like. These were Central Americans. Like I said, Guatemalans or El Salvadorans: They would say: hin, cheekun, torteeya.

"They drove us from the house, like prisoners... threatened with machine guns... escorted. Just the males. Some people from town looked at us, said hello to us, as if worried. Others as if pleased. They took us away around six in the morning to a house under construction, by the market. At about four in the afternoon the huge cloud of smoke. 'What could these bastards be burning,' I wondered. They'd set fire to all the family cars, my sons-in-law's, my daughters'... seven cars in all. And all our belongings. Just horrible. I said to a female major, the one who was guarding us, 'what have I ever done to you people! Why us? What do you people want? What have we ever done to you, you foreigners?' 'We want war, war, war!' is all she answered.

"The ringleader arrived, a guy named Mario, I think. I told him to try me already if they were going to kill me. 'All the rich are going to die for being exploiters.' And I told him: 'Look, you bastard, bring anybody from town to see if they accuse me... that landing strip, that school named after my mother, that athletic field named after my brother. Me, I grow beans, maize, work the field, plant on a large scale.' And he went on and on. He brought out his list of rich people: Mario Balboa, Alfredo Espinoza, José Solórzano, José Barragán, Adalberto López, Pepe Tárano, Marcelino Alcázar, about 15 or 20.' That's my whole point, bastard, you guys don't even know this town. All those people except one have been dead for many years now!' I told him. 'But their descendants must still be here,' he answered. 'Well, sure, but everyone is responsible for their own actions: I can't deny what I have, but I've worked for it. Sure, I've got a few bucks. If you want to kill me for that, go on, then! Kill me and let the others go free. These guys, why do they have to pay for me? This one's a locksmith, he makes keys in San Cristóbal; this other one's an eye doctor, he's a university professor; this other one's a travel agent. What can you accuse them of? He didn't know what to say: 'I don't give a fuck. They're family members. They're going to die.'

"The ringleader left. A while later he came back. 'You're time's up,' he said. They lined us up. Got us ready for the firing squad. 'Ready!' My cousin Luis was already breaking down. 'Don't break down, Luis; we're not going to give them the satisfaction of seeing us in a bad light,' I told him. 'Aim!' Then someone came and whispered in his ear. 'Saved your asses, motherfuckers,' he said. Someone from the government arrived. He spoke with them, on behalf of the Governor. It was drizzling. They had us standing up all night. Me, I'm diabetic. My son-in-law, the doctor, got two chairs. He had to beg them to let me sit down. This was on January 2nd.

"To the Governor's envoy they'd said: 'tell the Governor to fuck himself.' And we go: 'We know the Army's gonna intervene.' 'If the Army does intervene, you guys will be the first ones dead.' A journalist managed to sneak in. He interviewed me. They almost didn't let him. When they let me go that same journalist came back again.

"When they would say something to me, I'd answer back. I became fearless, as I said before. I considered myself dead already. They would insult me, and I would insult them, too. My son-in-law, the one from Mexico City, a big guy, fat, a real chatterbox under other circumstances, told me: 'enough already, father-in-law, don't say anything else to them. Be quiet now father-in-law. You keep quiet.' And I go: 'Why should I be quiet?'

"About noon many of the gunmen left with their leader, the guy named Mario. They took us to the marketplace. That female major stayed behind guarding us. She spent the whole time caressing her machine gun, an impressive weapon, brand new, and said to her subordinate: 'Look, this black beauty hasn't tasted any meat; today she's going to do it for the first time'; and after a little while, once again stroking her machine gun and telling her female captain: 'This black beauty hasn't drunk blood. But today she's going to do it for the first time.'

"A little later a helicopter came and the major shouted orders to her people: 'Wherever it lands, finish them off. Don't leave a single one alive. Waste them all.' The helicopter approached very close but didn't descend. The broad shouted: 'Everybody ready. Just let them get closer.' The helicopter went off toward the second valley. After a while, about an hour later, we saw it coming near the end of the camp. It came in flying at almost ground level. The major saw it, and started giving orders: 'That's it, everybody ready; don't leave a single one alive. Now!' And the shooting started. The soldiers fell out of the helicopter one by one. 'Don't leave even one alive!', the major kept yelling and everybody was shouting for joy. Around 10 soldiers fell out, and the Zapatistas were whooping and hollering. 'That's it! Send us some more of those!' And all those soldiers who fell to the ground, as if dead, they weren't dead. There were about 10 of them. They were hurling themselves on the landing strip, they were hurling themselves in the middle of that living hell. And just those 10 soldiers finished off little by little the 60 or 80 Zapatistas from the marketplace... just those 10 that the Zapatistas men and women thought they'd killed.

"Us, as soon as the shooting started, we hit the deck without realizing it. They'd put us on the front line. There, sprawled out on the ground we saw people fall dead and heard shots whizzing over our heads. Nearby me, I could see some cement blocks, two of them. I laid one flat on its side and stood the other on end and that's where I put my head. The firestorm continued from both sides. Suddenly, pow! the block shattered over my head! I felt my hair full of brick dust. I stood the other block up on end. I pressed myself against the ground. And a little while later pow! the other block shattered! Now I had nothing to protect myself with. I put my head on a little edge of one of the market stalls and stayed still, there. Motionless. Suddenly a scream: it was my son-in-law, the great big one: 'I'm fucked! They shot me!', he screamed. My other son-in-law, Talango, the doctor, checked him over. There was nothing wrong with him. It was just a scratch. He's so big and huge that even lying down he was raised very high up off the ground and the bullet had grazed pure fat. A little while later another scream. It was Luis Pascasio. Same thing, a flesh wound. Next the same son-in-law, the fat one: another flesh wound on his back. To this day, his wounds still haven't finished healing. 'Hang in there, guys... it doesn't matter... we'll see what happens!, I told them. Suddenly, during the shootout, a loud thundering sound and I felt the tremendous impact back here. 'That's it. I'm done for', I thought. But no. The impact had pierced the marketplace sheet metal and a burning sliver had fallen on top of me. I brushed myself off and saw that nothing was wrong. Only now my butt was burning! About four hours went by like that. There was a moment when they were running out of ammo. The major was demanding a doctor and left her machine gun unattended, right there, about two or three yards away. I felt the urge to take it. I was about to do just that when the major was also wounded, too. Out of ammo and wounded. A grenade that blew a hole in the marketplace wall saved them. They started escaping through there.

"Night fell. When nobody was talking any longer, we started shouting: 'Don't shoot! We're civilians. Don't shoot!' And I told my son-in-law, the great big one, who had more lung power: 'Go on, you bastard, yell!' And he goes: 'I can't. I can't. I can't...' He was dumbstruck! We kept shouting, 'we're civilians!', over and over again until the soldiers responded. 'Come out with your hands up!' Nobody wanted to go out. 'Come out with a white handkerchief!' Finally I went out. One by one they took us away with the general. When he found out who I was, he said to me, 'Ahh, so you're don Enrique Solórzano! For the moment, you're famous everywhere! They've spoken very highly of you to us. Good thing you're OK. Stay here, lie down; for the present you're our prisoner.' He ordered a medic to look me over, a doctor from Guadalajara. Now this was taking place in what was his headquarters, his offices. I didn't know where I was. The doctor gave me a tranquilizer. I said I was fine, but he gave it to me anyway. About five or ten minutes later, I realized we were in Adolfo Miguel's house. That's where headquarters was; there we were. They put us under the curtain, in that warehouse of Adolfo Miguel's. That's where the general was. My son-in-law, the travel agent, convinced people from the Red Cross to give us a blanket. And then, sure; we laid down to sleep. I'd never slept beside a man, but there I sure did... to sleep!

"My wife and my daughters, first they'd held them in a small room. There they brought them food, family members or servants.

"The next day, when they freed me, I went upstairs to Adolfo's house. It was empty. We changed clothes, took a bath, found some of Alfonso's clean clothes. My son-in-law, the great big one, found a huge hunk of cheese and some stiff tortillas. Umm, very tasty! We ate Adolfo's huge hunk of cheese.

"I saw about 50 dead bodies. My brother had arranged for a helicopter, my son from Villahermosa likewise. On January 5th the general told me: 'Alright, then... where do you want me to send you?' In an Army vehicle they carried me off to Carmelita's, my daughter-in-law's house. I sent a message to my wife through him. That's the only way she agreed to come. They'd already told her I was OK, but she didn't believe it. Until she got my message. Then the questions started: 'And Francisco?' Francisco Talango, the eye doctor. Nothing. We knew nothing. He ran off from the marketplace that day. And then there were so many dead bodies. He was wearing a green jacket. At around six in the evening of January 5th, already unrecognizable, he was found. They recognized him by his class ring and because of a small cross that he was wearing.

"An Army doctor told me lots of people died. 15 helicopters removed dead bodies: let's just suppose 10 per trip. Lots of people.

"I wouldn't go back now. I'm old already. I'm a rancher but I've had enough.

ARMANDO TORRES

The Torres brothers have spent their lives on the ranches "down yonder," as the ranches of the Second Valley are known. San Antonio, San Lorenzo, Santa Catarina, Tecojá, El Real, El Rosario, La Victoria... around those parts they have paraded their capacity as great cowboys, as horsemen, as ranchers who know their stuff.

Armando Torres Solís is 62 now. By the fruit of his labor overseeing ranches and caring for others' livestock, he succeeded in buying his first little plot of land 28 years ago. "62 acres that we bought from don Pepe Tárano, fields from El Real." That first little ranch was called San Martín de Porres. "Now finally, with more years of effort I had me another ranch also adjacent to El Real. It had 383 acres and used to be called San Martín Caballero."

I talk with Armando Torres on a bench in Tuxtla's central park, in September of 1994, during the ranchers' sit-ins demanding justice. Just as we're about to start our conversation, another rancher approaches and says something to Armando. When Armando returns he tells me: "They were already wanting to get on my case. Saying don't I know it's dangerous to talk with reporters. It's because reporters see us as enemies, are on the bad guys' side, paint a bad picture of us, don't see us as laborers. But I already told him I'm not talking to a reporter but to a writer who's from my hometown, a friend of mine. I know who to talk to and who not to, I said."

The legend of these men on horseback lured me ever since I was a kid. Seeing Armando in Tuxtla, so out of his rancher element, I wanted to talk with him. I introduce myself. He identifies me. In the first sentences Rubén Rodríguez' name comes up, another of the great cowboys from "down yonder," my uncle, passed away some 20 years ago it must be. Armando rejoices thinking back on uncle Rubén. Says, "Rubén and I loved each other like brothers." Then tells this story:

"The first one who came along with ideas of armed uprising was Eloy Cardel, about 20 years ago. He came with a letter of recommendation from don José Solórzano. Came with a group of people. They'd already tricked don José. He asked us to take care of the gentlemen, saying they were going to do business: that they were interested in buying sweet potatoes. A pack of lies: same as when they came up to my brother who was working another ranch. Him they told they were chili pepper traders, not sweet potato traders. At El Rosario they said they were coming to buy barbasco root.[109]

"So, they came and we attended to them. Their leader arrived. His name was Ángel López. They started promising us things. Sent us a doctor Saturdays and Sundays. A total of 35 men came. They told us they were going to put in dryers for us at the waterfall. I had a nephew of mine who's a baker, used to bring stuff to them at Agua Azul.[110] Because soon afterwards they holed up in the hills of Agua Azul and were living there, in some caves. They looked after each other and looked out for each other. They would only come out on the weekend. They also set up like a little school for the kids. One of them, a teacher, taught classes. Well, sure enough, one day when my brother Adán's wife was about to give birth we went to see them. We shouted out to them and, to give you an idea of how they looked after each other, we shouted to them and didn't hear a thing. Suddenly they appeared behind us, well armed and without making a sound.

"Another time my brother's son was going to be baptized and the priest from Ocosingo didn't want to come. Ángel López told me not to worry, that he had a priest and would bring him pronto. He did indeed bring him. They had everything.

"Then rumors started running around. The head of the school district passed by to tell us don't send the children to those men, that it was dangerous, that they were communists. Saturday, when the teacher arrived, the families didn't send the children to him. The doctor, yeah him they let work. Four days later when Ángel López arrived he was very angry, said they were going to see what he was really made of, that school district head was going to die. Ángel López always carried around a lot of money. As if by accident he would leave his jersey lying around with the money, so people would see it.

"One time planes came to collect everything. They went off to Taniperlas, like running away. We didn't find out anything else. But soon after we heard on the radio that Cardel was under arrest, that he was under arrest because he was crazy. My brother heard it on the radio. Next a helicopter arrived. People gathered around. Since we weren't guilty, we gathered together to talk. There was a short, heavyset guy who seemed familiar. I was telling the newcomers: 'Hope you aren't gonna turn out to be sweet potato traders,' I was saying; the short, heavyset guy just bowed his head. Suddenly the short fat guy says to me: 'What do you sleep on?' 'On tree limbs, sticks and a bedroll,' I answered. 'We'll see, let's have a look.' So, we went. There he identified himself: the Federal Prosecutor.

"They went to call my brother. They told him it was about some lumber merchant, or who knows what. Nothing. It was because of that Cardel business. He told us there was no problem with us. And there wasn't. Us, we used to work measuring La Victoria, parceling it out. They left and came back again. They took us to La Victoria, but the Prosecutor's Office had left me an address just in case they were bothering us.

"They took us to Tenosique by helicopter, then to Villahermosa. The judges arrived. We went to eat. Weren't in the mood. We were being detained, something like that. That's where I lapsed back into the cigarette habit I'd kicked a while before. The next day we went to a big conference room. They read us my declaration. Showed us pictures of the doctor and the oft-mentioned Ángel López. They showed me the photographs, and asked me if I knew them. And I told them, this one is the doctor and this is Ángel López. 'No way that's Ángel López! 'No!' This one's name is Mario Menéndez!', said the leader of those who were interviewing me.

"Well, that was a while back. Then more recently I worked on a road leading to Las Tazas and the ones who're now with Zapatistas passed by to offend me, to insult me. They were

Father Vicente's people: a guy who ran off and is with the Zapatistas in La Nueva Estrella.

"That happened. Then some of my godsons passed by to tell me I should tell people in Ocosingo they were armed. Afterwards, on May 3, 1994, they kidnapped me and took me to Nuevo Tuxtla. They held me without charge in a jail, sleeping on a tire. All because a boy bought 50 acres and the Zapatistas took 25 from him. He came to file a complaint with the prosecutor. He want back and cut the fence wire, fired some shots. He told them someone from the agricultural reform department was going to come take the measurements. He had them arrest one of the Zapatista leaders. And for that they came to tie *me* up. Until they released the Zapatista under arrest in Ocosingo, they weren't releasing me. But why me? Who knows... that's how they are. In the end, my brothers organized and pressured the authorities till they set me free.

"This last time I warned representative Octavio Albores two months before. He thought I was crazy, a gossipmonger. After everything that happened, I complained to him because he hadn't believed me. Octavio Albores said it wasn't him; that motherfucking governor was the one who said I was lying.

"I had three barbecues in December. In Ocosingo on the 16th or 17th, then in Bachajón, then in Pantelhó. When I came back they were already stopping cars. On the 31st I was wishing the commandant Happy New Year" when they came to tell him: 'Let's go, people with guns have arrived.'

"They had their training camp in Cedral de Ibarra. Sometimes, when the priest would come to a rural settlement, I'd be hired to prepare a barbecue. But I had to serve it outside that meeting area. They wouldn't allow access to their get-togethers.

"I'm Catholic but I don't like going to mass: they just blame it all on the ranchers. A little while ago the bishop was there and a Spaniard who already left.

"Now here we are. All that work for someone else's benefit.

"With my deceased wife I had a family of nine. Now I've gotten together with a new woman. I'm 62 and she's 22. As they say around these parts, "for an old cat, a tender mouse.""

DOÑA CELINA^{III}

Doña Celina, my mother, daughter and granddaughter of ranchers, is speaking:

"Well, around here, the first person who started with that land reform business was old Plácido Flores. He was from the village of Venustiano Carranza, one of those no-good Carranzans; like so, short, stocky and half-black, exactly like the Zapatistas. (Some people said he was from Guerrero, or from Belize or from someplace in Central America. Who knows.)[112]

"He came to Ocosingo to live, around 1926 I think, or before. He married—no, not even married—kidnapped aunt Teresa Martínez and went to ask for lodging and work at El Paraíso. Uncle Cuauhtémoc took him in, gave him work and gave him the great big room to live in, that big room that always used to be empty, there in the main house at El Paraíso. In the beginning he was working well and was living there because uncle Cuauhtémoc felt sorry for aunt Teresa, who was part of the family. Old Plácido used to be called "the pleated pant" because of some huge pleated pants he used to wear. Ah, but he was really nasty, the lousy old man. Every day, he made it a point to give poor aunt Teresa a beating. But a savage beating: he used to leave her face all bumped and bruised. All because they had a little girl about three years old, Chabela Flores, who went to wait for him at the corral gate and complained to him that her mom had hit her. And since la Chabela was just as ugly as the old man, he loved her dearly. That was the pretext.

"This began to bother uncle Cuauhtémoc.

"Also, jealous old Plácido started rabble-rousing the Indians: they all began working less. El Paraíso used to be beautiful then. There were lots of people. The Indians' houses were clean and neat, pretty, all of them gathered around the big house. And it was cheerful: during the festival of Dolores traders' tents used to arrive from Altamirano, from Comitán, from San Cristóbal. El Paraíso was extremely big. It bordered on El Real and Tecojá. It was already big in and of itself but grew more when aunt Constancia and uncle Cuauhtémoc got married. Dolores belonged to aunt Constancia. By the way, don Espiridión and papa Juan didn't get along. They had problems over land boundaries, or because the cattle would wander from one side to the other. In the end, they didn't know their children would get married. So the quarrels ended and El Paraíso and Dolores together grew much more. Who knows how many acres they had: about 20,000 or 25,000 maybe.

"Around that time uncle Cuauhtémoc sold off his property. He sold all of Rancho Nuevo México to the Alcázar family; also, to the Castellanos, all of Rancho Tijuana. All that used to be part of Dolores, in other words, used to belong to aunt Constancia.

"Well, of course uncle Cuauhtémoc, seeing how mean the old man was to aunt Teresa, and seeing how he stirred up the Indians, started thinking how to kick him out of there. He decided to give him a field that used to be part of El Paraíso. And they went to live there. He gave him permission to build a house, to harvest timber from Dolores, to take cedar for his doors and even gave the old bastard a property deed. And his reward was lies and slander. The old geezer starting turning people against him, convinced almost all the Indians to go with him, told them they were going to start a village. They did. A collective the old man called Puertobelo. It still exists. Very few people remained on El Paraíso: the Jiménez family, their great-grandparents from el Miguel. And also don José Paniagua, Pepe's father, who was a very good man, very hard-working, very responsible. Old Plácido hated those who refused to go along him with him. One day when there were no brown sugar cones, don José Paniagua went out on horseback to look for some. He went over in that direction, looking around, asking around for brown sugar. Well, as soon as old Plácido found out he was around, he ordered the Indians to kill him. And they hacked him to death with machetes. Wouldn't let his family pick up the body. The corpse decomposed there four days, till the state police came to pick it up. They didn't let the men from El Paraíso enter with the police. Only women could come through.

"Things like that the old man did, till they killed him many years later. They blamed uncle Cuauhtémoc and other ranchers he'd harmed. And the thing about it is that those damned land reformers came not to the national lands but to already developed ranches, which were already cultivated, which were already producing. That's what they're always looking for, like all good-for-nothings.

"So, that's how it all got started. Since then land reform started to be talked about, with that rotten old man. Now, there's even a town named Plácido Flores; there, too, in the Second Valley.

"For a long time, uncle Cuauhtémoc went around with the threat hanging over his head: 'today, they're gonna kill you', 'tomorrow they're gonna kill you'; like that, for a long time and all alone there, holed up in the jungle. But uncle Cuauhtémoc was a very brave man. There he remained, with his rifles and sons and sons-in-law, ready to defend their ranch.

"One day, some men holed up at Dolores, which used to have little red-tiled houses, whitewashed, very pretty. The Indians arrived and holed up in the houses, some tiled and some thatched and stayed there. Then uncle Cuauhtémoc, very early next day, was already kicking them out. They kicked them out of the tiled houses and chopped the thatched ones down with machetes. Uncle Cuauhtémoc was already back at El Paraíso around 10 o'clock, happy now because he'd kicked them out. They didn't kill anybody but they did drive them out.

"The Indians are so no-good they even wanted to steal the Madonna. In the chapel at Dolores there was always the Virgin, a big sculpture, made out of wood, which aunt Constancia's parents brought from Guatemala when her parents died. She took the Virgin from the little church at Dolores to the Oratory at El Paraíso and said that when she died they could return it to the chapel. That's how it was done. When aunt

Constancia died, aunt Consuelo, who inherited Dolores, gave it back. Then, when the Indians took aunt Consuelo's land away from her, they wouldn't let her remove the Virgin. But finally she was able to. Now Our Lady of Dolores stands in the Oratory of her house in San Cristóbal. And the Indians already looted El Paraíso and Dolores. Now supposedly they're venerating some image of old Samuel, [113] who's the one that taught them how to steal."

LA TONA

La Tona is an indigenous Tzeltal[114] who was widowed
when her daughters were still little girls. She is from Sivacá.
After the death of her husband, she came to Ocosingo to
live. She spends every day, from six in the evening on, selling
the delicious tamales she makes throughout the day: banana
leaf tamales; round, pork-rib tamales; guaán plant tamales;
Mexican pepperleaf (*mumo*) tamales; chipilín tamales; chicken
tamales; sweet tamales; vegetable tamales, etc. This she did,
does and will do, let us hope, for some time to come. I recall
the image of the beautiful woman 25 years earlier: tall, haughty
and fine, a bronzed, lovely creature with a mane of jet black
hair, an indigenous beauty typical of Sivacá. By the fruits of
her labor, she bought a piece of land, and built her house. Her
daughters grew up, and are as hard-working as their mother.
La Tona comes during these "postwar days," and asks with a
preoccupation that almost makes her cry: 'Doña Celinita... I
don't know whether to ask or not to ask; it's just that I'm so
scared; but can it really be true that we're no longer Mexicans?
Some of those men, they were saying that the government's
already sold us off to the gringos. Sold everything. Sold
Palenque, even![115] That now we belong to them. What're they
gonna make us do? They say that's what the guerrillas are
fighting for. That that's why they'd come to kill people. My
daughter's had to go to work at the medical office, and, poor
thing, every day she goes in shaking like a leaf and comes back
like this: shaking like a leaf, poor thing! Me, I can't even sleep,
doña Celinita. During those days, everybody was sleeping with
me, my daughters and my grandkids. I looked like a mother
hen, if only you'd seen it. I think those guerrilla fighters are
from Hell. And now you can't even go to church anymore to
put yourself in God's hands, because those priests are no good
anymore, they're no help. Who's gonna believe them?'

LA MARCELINA

La Marcelina is another one of the women everybody in town knows.

She sells pozol, tostadas, tortillas, pinole[116], memelas[117], and all the treats made from corn.

She goes from house to house with her payload.

I hear her telling the story, in the kitchen: "If only you'd a seen it, me, I wasn't even scared when the guerrillas came to town. I even went and had a little talk with some of 'em.

"And you guys, so what do you want?, I asked them.

"We're gonna confiscate rich people's property.

"Aw, fuck! What good's that gonna do? Don't tell me you don't know how to work. Well, you got hands. Or maybe you're cripple. The rich have what they have 'cause they worked for it. Besides, some rich people are good people, help people. There's also rich folks that are bastards, but what's theirs is theirs. I'm not gonna go and rob 'em. Me, maybe I feel like goin' 'round robbin' or beggin.' I'm alone, and I work and support my little children.

"But us, we don't have nothing.

"Well, didn't I just tell you you got hands? That's what God gave you hands for, to work, not just scratch your nuts with.

"That's what I was telling 'em when I see right then and there that they're killin' the commandant! Feets, don't fail me now! I didn't go out sellin' no more till them soldiers came! Them, they buy lots of stuff off me. That's why I even made their tamales for them. Two buckets full of mini-tamales I brought 'em. They used to go down good on those drizzly days. I just feel bad for 'em, out there sufferin' for our sake."

DON TONITO

Don Antonio Meza Ballinas, don Tonito, as he is known to the community of ranchers in the first and second valley, inherited from his father, don Antonio Meza, both the name and the El Recreo ranch. A respectable and well-loved family, don Tonito's. Son of doña Aurelia, grandson of don Cuauhtémoc, great-grandson of don Juan Ballinas (the man who, in the second half of the 19th century, explored the course of the Jataté River and named rivers, lagoons, mountains and valleys in this part of the world). Don Tonito speaks. This is the story of his house, of his hard work, of his name:

"El Recreo is a subdivision of Dolores. Dolores belonged to my grandmother Constancia, who married my grandfather Cuauhtémoc Ballinas. My mother received this land when she married, and my father built the ranch by the sweat of his brow. When my parents got married, they were living in Dolores. El Recreo used to be nothing but virgin forest. There were deer, porcupines, wild boar, yellow-crowned parrots, the lowland paca or spotted cavy, crested guan birds, spider monkeys and howler monkeys. All that disappeared about 20 years ago. Anyway, all of that was there when my father came to build El Recreo.

"My father built the ranch with a pair of oxen his godfather Marcelino Alcázar had rented him. To make a ranch produce takes a lot of work. All the more so when you have to start by clearing the land. Even more so if the plot is a huge woodland area. While my father was working during this initial phase, a snake bit one of the oxen and killed it. Just think how much snake venom it takes to kill an ox. My father was worried. He went and asked how much the ox was going to cost him. 'For you, my godfather,' don Marcelino replied, '150 pesos.'[118] My father went back home worried, and told my mother. She cried. She knew that the pair of oxen, the both of them, had cost don Marcelino 100 pesos. She knew it because an uncle of hers had been the seller. But oh, well. My father paid up.

But another gentleman, Pepe Tárano, got wind of the story: he gave my father two oxen, and didn't charge him a cent. It takes all kinds. That's how El Recreo started.

"My father built his little house using wattle and daub construction (walls of sticks and mud). It was about 33 feet long. About 10 years later, he made a 13-foot addition to it, out of adobe. Then another 13-foot addition and two corridors, 10 feet each on either side. The house is on a small hill, and toward the south you could see the hill of El Paraíso and part of the second valley; to the north, a landscape of big trees: only jungle. Many years later, around about 1967, the wattle and daub part changed to brick, brick made at the ranch. We brought the bricklayer in along with his laborers all the way from San Cristóbal. It was beautiful. Since there were lots of wild animals around, their footprints were imprinted on the wet brick: claws, small talons, tiny paw-prints and hoofs. When I was a boy, you would go from El Recreo to El Paraíso and there wouldn't be a single village. Now there are lots of settlements and small ranches.

"The old house was made with wild mahogany posts. Over the years, some of the wooden posts got eaten away, and I swapped them for wild tamarind wood. Finally, three years ago, we put up chains and concrete support beams. At that time, there was already a way of transporting materials over an unpaved road. The house turned out really nice, with its colonial look. I have pictures of how the house was in the beginning and now. The photos are all I have left.

"I was born on El Recreo. My parents and grandparents were born there. I have been tied to my land more spiritually than materialistically. I lived there all my life, except for a few years. My ancestors lived there. They're buried there. I'd be lying if I said I lived there because of my children, for the sake of my family, out of necessity. It's not like that: I lived there because I liked living there. I had the chance to live in a large or medium-size city or small town and have a ranch hand taking care of the place, but no. I didn't have a caretaker: I took care of my ranch. And not for business or profit, or as an investment; but because of being rooted in the land, out of love for the land where I was born. Sometimes I think I sacrificed my family, but they say no: they liked ranch life; the ones that went away to school used to spend their vacations there; loved their land, like me.

"When we were kids, the only teacher we had was our mother. From her, we learned to read and write. She would teach us while my father did the field work. Sometimes we'd already be asleep by the time he got back home. The education we got was good. When it came time to leave home and study in San Cristóbal, I started out in third grade.

"We inherited the land from my mother. Three ranches came out of it: Jahuaca, which belongs to my sister Socorro; El Tepeyac, which belongs to my sister Maria Natalia; and El Recreo, which is my property. Jahuaca was named after a plant called jahuacté that used to grow everywhere. It used to be virgin territory, with lots of cedar, monkeys, wild animals. Governor Velasco Suárez seized those lands and forced the vegetation to be destroyed, 'because it was unproductive land.'

"As I said before, El Tepeyac, the other subdivision of El Recreo, belonged to my sister Maria Natalia. She and her husband César built their house there; they've invested in their ranch but live in San Cristóbal. They're both teachers.

"El Recreo became mine: 475 acres. I'm not ambitious. I derive satisfaction from being able to support my family, my children. I have worked the land. One of my sons works with me. The two of us and five other employees, two of my godsons among them. People who were always with me.

"During the long days of June and July, I would get up at 5:30 in the morning; in December, one hour before daybreak. On waking up, you'd have coffee, some refried beans, home-made bread. And off to work. I work the livestock or the tractor. Cattle ranching consists of disinfecting livestock against ticks, according to the season. During the rainy season the cattle aren't taken to the pens, on account of the mud. The cows get stuck and the yearling calves even break bones. The cows would be checked over just as they were about to give birth, you'd see to it that they were healthy, that they didn't have problems. When the cattle were taken to the pens, they'd be given salt, branded, and were treated.

"Before 1970 it was very hard to herd cattle. You had to drive them toward Teopisca, in Chiapas, or all the way to Tenosique, in Tabasco. Seven days on horseback over muddy roads, at the mercy of inclement weather, of wild animals, of swollen rivers. You slept out in the open, on a rain cape, with your saddle for a pillow. Herds were small: 50 head of cattle. Sometimes buyers would come scouring the ranches to buy up livestock. And that's how it was. The roads the cattle were herded over were difficult, muddy, narrow, bad. But people were good: there was always support, and we were well received at the ranches during nightfall; we paid, of course, but we were well received everywhere we went.

"The work was hard but we were hard workers.

"When the highway reached Ocosingo, in 1970, we started herding large livestock from there; wonderful: only three days' ride from the ranch. A huge advantage. Then the road reached Toniná and Guadalupe, a few years later, around 1980. Another advantage: now we were starting the cattle off from there, in Guadalupe, only two days' ride. Finally, the Pemex highway arrived in 1992. Now we would drive the cattle two hours from the ranch, alongside the highway. With effort, with my own money, I struggled as hard as I could to build a bridge. We succeeded. I took part in the construction of the bridge over the Naranjo River. We did it back when Alfredo Díaz was mayor of Ocosingo. That bridge is still in use to this day.

"In 1981, I had a tractor. We got it on credit. Before the tractor, the method of cultivating the land was the old slash-and-burn system. Only two people in the second valley had tractors, Captain Javier Castellanos and I. When I was working the tractor, it was an all-day thing. My little ones would bring food to me out in the field, would bring me water to wash up with, would bring me lunch and pozol. I used to have lunch in the field at 8 or 9 in the morning. At 2 I'd drink the pozol, and finish my chores at about five in the afternoon. I'd bathe: a good-sized river, the Naranjo River runs through

El Recreo's lands. Also a stream, the Tzapaltón, which means 'buried stone.' In the river or in the stream I'd bathe and then go back home a little before five to put diesel in the tractor. My wife would help me with this. On hearing the noise, she'd go out to the fence to wait for me and help me change the diesel so as to avoid condensation. She'd give me clean clothes. Afterwards, I'd have coffee; and so to bed. There was no electricity. At first I had two kerosene lamps, then gas. Day was done at 8 o'clock. At that hour, we'd all be asleep already. That's what typical days were like from Monday to Saturday.

"In 1985, we had a battery-operated television.

"Since getting the tractor I was able to fertilize and reap corn harvests of four tons per 2.5 acres. With slash-and-burn you can't even reap one. All this production was for our own consumption, because it was very expensive to take it to market. I'd sell the corn here and there, whatever was left. The corncob was for the cattle. With the tractor and a terracer blade that I bought for it, I could make or maintain the road.

"This has been my life. I'm 54 years old. I went away to school for a few years. I got as far as UNAM.[119] I was studying to be a petroleum engineer but, because of my father's illness, I came back to take charge of ranch in 1963. Here is where I fulfilled myself. I had four sons and one daughter that we adopted. The oldest is 28 years old, and the youngest 9. Another one of my sons, who's 26 and married now, lives in Monterrey. He's an agronomist. He has a little boy. He stayed on there.

"Leticia, my wife, always liked ranch life. She loved flowers. She used to tend her garden. She really loved the kitchen, trying out new dishes, entertaining guests. She would make bread in an oven we used to have, or in her 'miracle' molds. We finally got a freon gas refrigerator.

"Due to technical difficulties only beef cattle were raised.[120] I greatly improved the livestock: at first we raised about 50 head a year, as I said. Then, improving the pastures with the tractor, with better fodder and concentrates, we could have two animals per 2.5 acres. Thanks to the greater efficiency of the soil everything improved. At first we pastured bull calves that were 3 years old, then 30 months, then two-year-olds. And finally, during the last two years, we succeeded in pasturing one-and-a-half-year-old bulls weighing almost 1,000 pounds with excellent, tender meat. Reducing the average age increased the average yield. We used to produce two calvings a year.

"70 years after having started work on El Recreo, all this had improved: the house, the road, the tractor, the livestock. It seemed that the hard work of 70 years and three generations had finally paid off.

"Then the Zapatistas came along and stole everything.

"The problems started in 1975, when we were fighting for the highway. Three invasions occurred. They encroached on Takinás, don Mario Balboa's property. Then they invaded another plot of land: Tantiquil. Takinás they renamed 'El Salvador', and Tantiquil they called 'Nazareth.' That was in January 1975. There was another invasion at El Cacao, the property of Doctor Enrique Stapool, an Englishman who bought that land in order to preserve the jungle. He didn't want them cutting down trees. Engineer Andrade, the surveyor who did the demarcation, was telling me that, after the boundary markers were traced in order to define the property limits, Doctor Stapool refused to let them cut the trees down. Stapool paid him extra just to mark each tree with his square and not have to cut them down. 'All this cost him more money but he wouldn't let trees be cut down,' the engineer said. This seemed strange to him. He viewed Doctor Stapool as an eccentric, a little crazy. 'He doesn't want the jungle deforested.'

"So, the raider organizations first accused the Englishman of holding unproductive lands, then they burned his trees and now they invaded the plot of land. This was the work of the Catholic organizations. For about seven years they were satisfied with these takeovers, but in 1983 they remounted the invasions. Now it was the Union of Unions and the PST[121].[122] Everything had been populated already. They took over Banabil (now Nuevo Leon), don Marcelino Alacázar's place. They seized Las Champas, an indigenous cooperative; they invaded Jahuaca and a subdivision of Santa Catarina (now Macedonia). In the town of Sabintelá they confiscated La Peña, and people from the area overran La Estrella. President Echeverría filled this area up with colonizers. All this was just in the second valley. Then ARIC came along. They managed to seize two properties: Las Champas y Jahuaca. Agreements were signed. With a lot of money, the government succeeded in controlling the organization. The invaders withdrew from Jahuaca, but invaded again a little while later. The Union of Unions was appealed to in order to protest this violation of the agreements but they said that they had nothing to do with it, that the intruders were from another organization. In fact, the invaders identified themselves as CNPI.[123] They weren't Union of Unions anymore but the people were the same; they'd just changed labels, that's all! Fortunately the government drove them out. Jahuaca used to be an indigenous collective.

"From that point on calm ensued. Up until the recent outbreak.

"In Tecojá there were Guatemalan guerrillas moving about with complete freedom. They crossed into Mexico calmly, to those properties, with the Mexican government's permission, I think. They were working here. Then I found out that people from here were training in Pamalá, on La Estrella, but I never saw anything. I only learned about the outbreak eight days before. A good friend of mine, don Andrés Pérez, from the Union of Unions, told me, fearful of the training. Told me they were putting up fences and crawling underneath, that they were giving them military training. He told me this on December 24th, terrified. 'The war's gonna be worldwide... who knows,' he said. I almost believed him. He told me there'd been a clash between OCEZ[124] and the Union of Unions. I didn't say anything to the family, only to my brother-in-law César. I didn't want to frighten my family. I told my brother-in-law we should send a letter directly to Señor Patrocinio, the Governor of Chiapas. Andrés had told me war was coming, that the army would be unknown. When all was said and done, we didn't send the letter. We all stayed put at the ranch. On New Year's Day, my son was coming over to have supper with us. He arrived late. He lives near the crossing, and told us they were stopping people there. When he said they were commandeering vehicles and carrying armed forces to Ocosingo, the party died down: we slept uneasy. The following morning, when we turned on the radio, the proclamations were already on the air.

"They reached the ranch. We saw them passing along the road, civilians, asking about 'El Salvador.' (There was a guy named Salvador at La Estrella: short and heavy-set, with a thick beard, of mixed-race, heavily armed; with a radio over which he would report his movements to headquarters.) There were 14 of us at the ranch, three families, my wife's brothers. We were there till January 10th. At first, I didn't want to leave, but then the fear set in, because of what we were hearing and because of the helicopters and planes. Poor people started passing through, kicked off their property by armed insurgents. 'They're throwing everybody out, they're stealing everything, they want to press the men and boys into service, or they're threatening to kill them.' Where to go. There we were in our house, we had everything we needed, we had food, we had the river. Where were we gonna go? I don't have any property in Ocosingo, or in San Cristóbal, either, not in Tuxtla, not in Mexico City. But people started to get desperate, to become more afraid. My sisters-in-law came up with the idea of putting the letters 'S.O.S.', in the field. Some helicopters passed by and saw the letters. They made another pass, hovering overhead. I went out and signaled with my cowboy hat. Another one passed by. I waved for help. They descended a bit but didn't land. Which was only natural; they didn't know if it was a trap. Another one passed by, I signaled, it descended, went away. Yet another. And another. They were looking right at us. They were talking on the radio. They flew away. The women in the house were crying. There was no way to communicate with the outside world. I used to have radio equipment at the ranch, but it'd been burnt out by lightning strike in October. But three days later, when the threat was increasing, they came for us. 'You have five minutes!', the soldiers shouted. We all ran. I just grabbed a suitcase with documents. My daughter left barefoot. They airlifted us in three helicopters.

"On February 1st, the Zapatistas entered my ranch. They destroyed the doors. They ransacked the house. They stole everything, smashed stuff. They stole construction materials. And all the livestock: 500 head, counting the calves.

"There was never any bombing around here. The planes were just flying over.

"My son is in Ocosingo now: has a small truck. One of my godsons is also in Ocosingo: I helped him buy a little place, and he's a livestock inspector with Rural Development.[125] Another one is on a ranch.

"It's all over, finished. Everything's destroyed, absolutely. We're emotionally destroyed. We're all threatened. It's all looting, stealing. The only thing left for me to do is accept whatever happens.

"Supposing the government does pay, mentally I'm preparing myself for something else. I don't know. Monterrey, maybe. In the state of Tabasco, a field hand is looked upon as a decent man, as a person worthy of respect, as a noble, honorable man. In the south of Veracruz state it's very dignified to be a rancher, I understand. Here, the cattle man, the rancher, useful people, the man who produces food so that people in the cities may eat, is seen as a criminal, like a drug dealer. We can't walk with our heads held high. The journalists and the government only listen to murderers, to priests, to politicians. Us, we've herded cows, bred horses, cultivated farmland. We're right, we have ideas, but we don't know how to articulate them, express them, present them. We're clumsy when it comes to that. We're working men. We're not politicians.

"I think the countryside is the shield, for now. But when the farm falls to the Zapatistas, the city follows. Those people are fighting for power. They're not gonna stop. They lie and kill. Us, we raise animals so people can eat. Them, they manipulate men so politics can drink blood. I have nothing left. What my ranch once provided is all gone. I inspire a lot of confidence in my family, I tell them I have faith, that everything will work out. They lean on me, but I don't have a leg to stand on.

"Together with the other dispossessed ranchers we've been thinking about buying something together if they pay us, someplace where we can protect ourselves, someplace where we can be left alone. But we don't know if they're gonna pay us. Or how much. They keep putting us off and putting us off and putting us off. Now it's postponed yet again. They say, not yet. They say, maybe Monday; the commission this; yesterday that; that two representatives... they're working out the regulations.

"But nothing will ever be the same.

"My grandfather, my mother and I, we were all born on El Recreo. They say you own your land, but I don't think so. The land owns you. We work for it. We belong to it."

Don Antonio Meza Ballinas, don Tonito, salt of the earth, extends his strong working man's hand. His clear-eyed gaze is blurred by tears.

ENDNOTES

1   At midnight Saturday, 1 January 1994, the North American Free Trade
     Agreement (NAFTA) took effect. Simultaneously, the Zapatista
     Army of National Liberation (EZLN), a theretofore unheard of
     rebel group, springs from the Lacandon Jungle. Well aware that
     Chiapas was an isolated area with a fragile infrastructure, poor
     transportation network and rugged terrain, they storm Ocosingo
     (pop. 20,000) and five other towns.
         In Ocosingo, rumor had it that the Zapatistas overpowered a
     Mexican Petroleum Corporation (PEMEX) facility, capturing 1.5
     tons of dynamite, more than 10,000 detonators as well as a heavy
     truck. This rumor proved to be unfounded. They kill two policemen,
     occupy the town and take over town hall.

2   A widely sung left-wing anthem. It has been one of the most
     recognizable and popular songs of the socialist movement since the
     late 19th century, when the Second International (now the Socialist
     International) adopted it as its official anthem.

3   Falcón, Castro Bustos and Raúl León de la Selva and other *porros*
     were "gangs of political thugs and provocateurs supported by
     politicians of Mexico's powerful PRI party in its heyday." Alberto
     Ulloa Bornemann: *Surviving Mexico's Dirty War: A Political Prisoner's
     Memoir.*

4   José de Jesús Núñez Molina, Mexican singer-songwriter of protest
     songs. Born Hermosillo, Sonora, in 1938. Creator of populist songs
     such as "Obreros y Patrones" and "Ayeres," among others.

5   Throughout the book, the author's wife, photographer Guadalupe
     Belmontes Stringel, is affectionately referred to by various
     nicknames: Pilla; Pillis; Pillita; Pita; Pía; and Pi.

6   Compañía Mexicana de Geofísica employed over 1,000 people in
     Chiapas, one of the poorest states in Mexico.

7   Ladinos are a socio-ethnic category of Mestizo or hispanicized
     people in Mexico and Central America. The demonym ladino came
     into use during the colonial era to refer to the Spanish-speaking
     population that did not belong to the colonial elite of *peninsulares* or
     criollos, nor to the indigenous peoples.

8   Amate is a form of paper that has been manufactured in Mexico
     since pre-Hispanic times. It was extensively produced and used for
     both communication, records and ritual during the Aztec Empire;
     however, after the Spanish conquest, its production was mostly
     banned and replaced by European paper.

9   October 12, 1993.

10 Instituto Mexicano del Seguro Social: Mexican Social Security Institute.

11 Author's note: director of PROCUP and later chancellor of the University of Oaxaca.

12 Partido Revolucionario Obrero Clandestino-Unión del Pueblo: Revolutionary Worker Clandestine Union of the People Party.

13 Partido de los Pobres: Poor People's Party.

14 Guerra Popular Prolongada: Prolongued Popular War.

15 Center of Agricultural Workers and Campesinos.

16 Emiliano Zapata Campesino Organization.

17 Peasant Alliance 'Emiliano Zapata.'

18 Alianza Nacional Campesina Independiente Emiliano Zapata: Emiliano Zapata Independent National Peasant Alliance.

19 Unión Nacional de Organizaciones Regionales Campesinas Autónomas (UNORCA): Union of Autonomous Regional Peasant Organizations.

20 Asociación Rural de Interés Colectivo (ARIC): Rural Association of Collective Interests.

21 National Peasant Confederation.

22 Instituto Chiapaneco de Cultura: Chiapas Cultural Institute.

23 Guadalupe's closest friend.

24 When the Zapatista uprising surprised the world in January 1994, the initial response of the Mexican government was to claim that it was the work of outside agitators — either Marxist guerrillas inspired by the Cubans or (equally left-wing) priests following the line of Liberation Theory. The bishop of Chiapas, Samuel Ruíz, was indeed an early convert to Liberation Theology, and the lay catechists his diocese recruited in the area where the Zapatista rebellion broke out sympathised with the emerging armed movement. Author's note: The Forces of National Liberation, origin of the EZLN, was a Marxist group, followers of Ché Guevara.

25 José Patrocinio González Blanco Garrido, ex-Governor of Chiapas (1988-1993); afterwards, Secretary of State for the Interior (1993-1994).

26 On Sunday, the fighting continues. Mexican federal forces are rapidly deployed in joint Army/Air Force operations. The police and Army attempt to recapture Ocosingo. 24 police officers are executed in surrounding towns, where helicopters and other aircraft fly overhead. Looting on the part of Ocosingo inhabitants is reported. Rebel forces free 120 inmates from a prison in San Cristóbal.

27 Instituto de Seguridad y Servicios Sociales de los Trabajadores del Estado: Institute for Social Security and Services for State Workers.

28 Tzeltal (or Ts'eltal) is a Mayan language spoken in the Mexican state of Chiapas, mostly in the municipalities of Ocosingo, Altamirano,

Huixtán, Tenejapa, Yajalón, Chanal, Sitalá, Amatenango del Valle, Socoltenango, Villa las Rosas, Chilón, San Juan Cancuc, San Cristóbal de las Casas and Oxchuc. As of 2005, it was a living language with some 371,730 speakers, including a number of monolinguals.

29 Party of the Democratic Revolution (*Partido de la Revolución Democrática*), a democratic socialist party in Mexico.

30 Toniná is a pre-Columbian archaeological site and ruined city of the Maya civilization located... some 8 miles east of Ocosingo, and some 40 miles south of the contemporary Maya city of Palenque, Toniná's greatest rival throughout its recorded history.

31 Acclaimed novella by Mexican author Agustín Yáñez. Published in English as *The Edge of the Storm* by University of Texas Press (1963).

32 *Juzgado Mixto de Primera Instancia*, a trial court that has multiple-forum jurisdiction over various subject matter cases, mainly civil and criminal.

33 Banco Nacional de México, or Banamex, Mexico's second largest bank.

34 Epiphany, January 6.

35 Chiclería refers to the commercial production of *chicle*, a natural resin base for chewing gum, which dominated the political economy of Central America for decades.

36 More than just colonists granted control of land and Indians to work for them, as in the U.S. indentured slave system, *encomenderos*, or grantees of an *encomienda*, were usually conquistadors and soldiers, but they also included women and native notables... Conquistadors were granted trusteeship over the indigenous people they helped conquer. The encomienda was essential to the Spanish crown's sustaining its control over North, Central and South America in the first decades after the colonization, because it was the first major organizational law instituted on a continent where disease, war and turmoil reigned.

The etymology of encomienda and encomendero lies in the Spanish verb encomendar, "to entrust." The encomienda was based on the [Spanish Reconquest] institution in which adelantados were given the right to extract tribute from Muslims or other peasants in areas that they had conquered and resettled. The [Latin American] encomienda system differed from the Peninsular institution in that Encomenderos did not own the land on which the natives lived. The system did not entail any direct land tenure by the encomendero; Indian lands were to remain in their possession. This right was formally protected by the Crown of Castile because at the beginning of the Conquest, most of the rights of administration in the new lands went to the crown. The system was formally abolished in 1720, but had lost effectiveness much earlier. In many areas it had been abandoned for other forms of labour. In certain areas, this quasi-feudal system persisted. In Mexico, for instance, it was not until the constitutional reform after the Mexican Revolution that the encomienda system was abolished, and the ejido became a legal entity again. (see also the history of the Chiapas conflict)

37 Berick Traven Torsvan. 1890-1969. US novelist, born in Germany and living in Mexico from 1920. His novels, originally written in German, include *The Treasure of the Sierra Madre* (1934); *La rebelión de los colgados* (1938) was translated into English as *The Rebellion of the Hanged* (1952).

38 Author and historian don Pedro Vega, better known as "Pablo Montañez."

39 An example of how hard it is to translate jokes. Author's note: "horse" refers to feminine towels used during the menstrual cycle. The Spanish text reads "cucaracha," which is a vulgarism for the vulva. The turn of phrase "I already brought her her hay" refers to her applying a great number of Kótex to her vulva (a herd of horses). See what we mean?

40 Author's note: This refers to the Villa de Guadalupe, a Catholic church sanctuary situated at the foot of Cerro del Tepeyac in Mexico City. It is the second most visited religious site in the world, surpassed only by St. Peter's Basilica, in Rome.

41 The Mexican Revolution was a major armed struggle that started in 1910, with an uprising led by Francisco Madero against longtime autocrat Porfirio Díaz, and lasted for the better part of a decade until around 1920. Over time the Revolution changed from a revolt against the established order to a multi-sided civil war. This armed conflict is often categorized as the most important sociopolitical event in Mexico and one of the greatest upheavals of the 20th century.

42 Frans Blom (August 9, 1893, Copenhagen—June 23, 1963, San Cristóbal de Las Casas, Chiapas, Mexico), Danish explorer and archaeologist.

43 Gertrude "Trudi" Duby Blom (1901—December 23, 1993), Swiss journalist, social anthropologist, and documentary photographer who spent five decades chronicling the Mayan cultures of Chiapas, Mexico, particularly the culture of the Lacandon Maya. In later life, she also became an environmental activist. Blom's former home Casa Na Bolom is a research and cultural center devoted to the protection and preservation of the Lacandon Maya and La Selva Lacandona rain forest.

44 Here, the author quotes a verse by Spanish poet St. John of the Cross (1542-1591).

45 Author's note: The indigenous peoples burn the original vegetation

to plant the corn fields.

46   Salvador Díaz Mirón (December 14, 1853—June 12, 1928) was a Mexican poet. He was born in the port city of Veracruz. His early verse, written in a passionate, romantic style, was influenced by Lord Byron and Victor Hugo. His later verse was more classical in mode. His poem, "A Gloria," was influential. His 1901 volume *Lascas* ("Chips from a Stone") established Mirón as a precursor of *modernismo*. After a long period of exile, he returned to Mexico and died in Veracruz on June 12, 1928.

47   Author's note: Center for Social Reinsertion, penitentiary.

48   Author's note: The excellent and justly famed bread from San Cristóbal.

49   Author's note: Not Uncle Sam but old Samuel, as the detractors of Bishop Samuel Ruiz were accustomed to call him.

50   On Monday, fighting escalates in Ocosingo. Former Chiapas governor, General Absalón Castellanos Domínguez, is kidnapped at his ranch by the EZLN, accused of crimes against Indians and other peasants. Chiapas state officials attempt to diffuse the situation by entering into dialogue with the EZLN. Rebels burn down the Ocosingo municipal building, and continue broadcasting from the captured radio station in heavy fighting throughout the day. The EZLN controls access to Ocosingo via roadblocks.

51   Carlos Salinas de Gortari (born April 3, 1948) is a Mexican economist and politician affiliated to the Institutional Revolutionary Party (PRI) who served as President of Mexico from 1988 to 1994.

52   José Patrocinio González Blanco Garrido, ex-Governor of Chiapas (1988-1993); afterwards, Secretary of State for the Interior (1993-1994).

53   Jacobo Zabludovsky Kraveski (born May 24, 1928) is a Mexican journalist. He was the first anchorman in Mexican television and his TV news program, *24 Horas* (*24 Hours*) was for decades the most important in the country. Mexican journalist Abraham Zabludovsky Nerubay is the son of Jacobo Zabludovsky. He worked as a television news anchor on *24 Horas de la Tarde* (1986—1988) and on *Abraham Zabludovsky en Televisa* (1998—2000). In 1991 he founded the weekly *Época*, which he edited until 1998.

54   Author's note: "ETA means Escuela Técnica Agropecuaria. CEBETA or CBTA means Centro de Bachillerato Tecnológico Agropecuario. These have nothing to do with the Basque terrorism."

55   Óscar Wong (Tonalá, Chiapas, agosto 26 de 1948), poet, narrator and essayist.

56   Professor Edgar Robledo Santiago. His literary works are numerous.

57   Juan Domingo Argüelles (born Chetumal, State of Quintana Roo, Mexico 1958), Mexican poet, essayist, literary critic, writer and

editor. He frequently contributes to the magazines *Libros de México*, *Quehacer Editorial* y *El Bibliotecario*, a CONACULTA publication.

58 Author and journalist born 1958 in Mexico City.

59 On Tuesday, there is heavy fighting in the town square. The Mexican Army recaptured the Ocosingo municipal buildings. But the EZLN, despite being cut off, would continue fighting, counter-attacking the Mexican Army advances with sniper fire from the outskirts of Ocosingo up until the cease-fire declaration of January 12.

60 Maseca is a popular brand of powdered corn meal.

61 "Pozol," in Chiapas, is the name given to a refreshing drink made from corn meal dissolved in water and seasoned with salt and green chilies. It is served cold, and is very much appreciated at midday when the heat is oppressive.

62 *Fernando Pessoa & Co.: Selected Poems*, Poem No. 32, page 58; Richard Zenith, translator.

63 Author's note: At that time, the exchange rate was 5,320 pesos to the dollar.

64 On Wednesday, in another Chiapas village, outraged townspeople ambush, bind and beat six rebel fighters, eventually turning them over to the Mexican Army. The road from Ocosingo to the Chiapas state capital is blocked off. 5,000 army soldiers in tanks and other armored vehicles converge on San Cristóbal, engaging EZLN forces with planes and helicopters along the highway that leads to Ocosingo. The Mexican Army recaptures Ocosingo, including the radio station. EZLN forces continue firing on federal troops.

65 XEOCH-AM, Ocosingo radio station. It forms a part of the Chiapas Radio, Televisión and Film Network.

66 Pinole is a Spanish translation of an Aztec word for a coarse flour made from ground toasted maize kernels, often in a mixture with a variety of herbs and ground seeds, which can be eaten by itself or be used as the base for a beverage. In southeastern Mexico and in Central America this food and beverage is known as *pinol* or *pinolillo*, considered the national beverage of Nicaragua.

67 There is a type of cookie in México called the "Maria" or collectively "Galletas Marías" that is almost considered to be a staple in the Mexican diet. The first solid food that Mexican babies eat is often a Galleta María dipped in milk.

68 Reference to Cuban poet Heberto Padilla's poem "Sobre los heroes," from his prize-winning collection *Fuera del juego* (*Out of the Game*). At once celebrated and castigated, Padilla was imprisoned by Fidel Castro's State Security forces in 1971. Sages, Padilla wrote, "Modifican a su modo el terror/Y al final nos imponen/la furiosa esperanza" (*Fuera del juego* 25) ("Modify terror in their own way/ and at last impose upon us/furious hope").

69 Jaime Sabines Gutiérrez (March 25, 1926 - March 19, 1999) was a
    Mexican contemporary poet. Known as "the sniper of Literature,"
    as he formed part of a group that transformed literature into reality,
    he wrote ten volumes of poetry, and his work has been translated
    into more than twelve languages. His writings chronicle the
    experience of everyday people in places such as the street, hospital,
    and playground... In 1995, his selected poems, *Pieces of Shadow* (trans.
    W.S. Merwin), was brought out in a bilingual edition by Papeles
    Privados; and in 2004 Exile Editions (Toronto, Canada) published
    a bilingual volume of three early Sabines books, *Adam and Eve* &
    Weekly Diary and *Poems in Prose* (trans. Colin Carberry). Octavio Paz
    considered him "one of the greatest contemporary poets of... [the
    Spanish] language."

70 Reference to the Jaime Sabines poem "Algo sobre la muerte del
    Mayor Sabines."

71 Quetzal, a Guatemalan monetary unit.

72 The Attorney General of Mexico (*Procurador General de la República*),
    head of the Office of the General Prosecutor (*Procuraduría General
    de la República*, PGR) and the Federal Public Ministry (*Ministerio
    Público de la Federación*), an institution belonging to the Federal
    Government's executive branch that is responsible for the
    investigation and prosecution of federal crimes.

73 *Instituto Nacional de Antropología e Historia* (National Institute of
    Anthropology and History) is a Mexican federal government
    bureau established in 1939 to guarantee the research, preservation,
    protection, and promotion of the prehistoric, archaeological,
    anthropological, historical, and paleontological heritage of Mexico.

74 *Instituto Nacional Indigenista* (INI), Mexico's (defunct) government
    agency for indigenous people.

75 On Thursday, EZLN rebels retreat from Ocosingo, but continue
    harassing Mexican Army soldiers with sniper fire.

76 Gabriel Bernal Vargas (5 February 1915-25 May 2010) was a Mexican
    painter, artist and cartoonist, whose comic strip *La Familia Burrón*
    was created in 1937. This cartoon has been described as one of the
    most important in Mexican popular culture. Vargas won Mexico's
    Premio Nacional de Periodismo (National Journalism Prize) in 1983 and
    the *Premio Nacional de Ciencias y Artes en el área de Tradiciones Populares*
    (National Sciences and Arts Prize) in 2003.

77 Gabriel Zaid (born 1934 in Monterrey, Nuevo León) is a Mexican
    writer, poet and intellectual. He was a member of the Board of
    Directors of Vuelta magazine from 1976 to 1992. His essays have
    been very influential on a vast array of topics, most significantly
    poetry, economics, and criticism of the literary establishment.

78 Ernesto "Che" Guevara (1928—1967), commonly known as el Che or simply Che, was an Argentine Marxist revolutionary, physician, author, guerrilla leader, diplomat, and military theorist. A major figure of the Cuban Revolution, his stylized visage has become a ubiquitous countercultural symbol of rebellion and global insignia within popular culture.

79 Allusion to Mexican author José Revueltas.

80 Quote from Salvador Díaz Mirón, from *Poesías*, Boston, Casa Editorial Hispano-Americana, 1895; from the Book Collection at Harvard University.

81 Author's note: Newly bought chickens enter into a new chicken coop and for a long while remain stationery and isolated, disconcerted.

82 Author's note: in psychoanalytic theory, reaction formation is a defensive process (defense mechanism) in which anxiety-producing or unacceptable emotions and impulses are mastered by exaggeration (hypertrophy) of the directly opposing tendency.

83 Nicanor Parra Sandoval (born 5 September 1914) is a Chilean mathematician and poet. He is considered an influential poet in Chile, as well as throughout Latin America. Some also argue he ranks among the most important poets of Spanish language literature... Nicanor Parra was born in 1914 in San Fabián de Alico, Chile, near Chillán, a city in southern Chile, the son of a schoolteacher. He comes from the artistically prolific Chilean Parra family of performers, musicians, artists and writers. His sister, Violeta Parra, is possibly the most important folk singer the nation has produced.

84 On Friday, a car bomb explodes at University Plaza in Mexico City. The Army establishes a perimeter around Ocosingo, Las Margaritas and San Cristóbal. Next, the Mexican Army goes on the offensive with infantry, armored vehicles, tanks, helicopters and other aircraft to force the EZLN from the area. The EZLN and Army continue to clash.

85 Author note: "*Nochig* is a Tseltal word referring to the plant *Lucuma salicifolia* o *Pouteria campechiana*." Sometimes also called the Maya fruit.

86 Quote from William Blake's "Proverbs of Hell," *The Marriage of Heaven and Hell*.

87 On Saturday, three Mexican Army airplanes and two helicopters are reported damaged by the EZLN. The Acapulco federal building, power lines and other infrastructure targets are bombed throughout Mexico. The EZLN denies any links to this terrorist activity.

88 In the prehispanic world, as well as in ancient Spain, parts of Africa, and a few other parts of the world, the weather that occurred during the first 12 days of January was believed to predict the weather for the

whole year. The period is called the Cabanuelas, from the Spanish word cabana or small cabin. The twelve cabanas house the weather. In modern Mexico, for those who have no grandparents closely tied to the land and agriculture, the term has lost its significance and now means only the rains that come in January.

89 *La Tremenda Corte* (*The Awesome Courthouse*) was a radio comedy show produced in Havana, Cuba. The scripts were written by Cástor Vispo, a Spaniard who became Cuban citizen. The show was aired nonstop from 1942 to 1961. Later, the format of the show was taken for a TV sitcom in Monterrey, Mexico, however, only three and a half seasons were produced from 1966 to 1969.

90 Sunday. The government attempts to restore basic services—electricity, water, sewage, gas—to towns recaptured by Army forces.

91 Mexican author.

92 Later, Governor of Chiapas.

93 Eraclio Zepeda, activist, story-writer and story-teller, media personality, is well remembered thanks to his appearance on the old channel 13, as presenter of "Canto, Cuento y Color." He is the author of *Benzulul*, *Trejito*, *Asalto Nocturno*, and *Andando el Tiempo*.

94 From "Romance de la Guardia Civil Española"/"Ballad of the Spanish Civil Guard"; spanish original: Los CABALLOS negros son./Las herraduras son negras./Sobre las capas relucen/manchas de tinta y de cera./Tienen, por eso no lloran,/de plomo las calaveras./Con el alma de charol/vienen por la carretera./Jorobados y nocturnos,/por donde animan ordenan/silencios de goma oscura/y miedos de fina arena.; English translation: Black are the horses./The horseshoes are black./On the dark capes glisten/stains of ink and of wax./Their skulls are leaden,/which is why they don't weep./With their patent-leather souls/they come down the street./Hunchbacked and nocturnal,/where they go, they command/silences of dark rubber/and fears like fine sand (A.L. Lloyd, translator).

95 On Monday, the Army attacks guerrillas holed up in Ocosingo. Isidro Guillermo Badillo Brana, a Mexican priest purportedly heading a guerrilla group, is captured at the Chiapas/Tabasco border. The Mexican stock market tanks. Mounting demonstrations in Mexico City and elsewhere. Former Chiapas governor and now interior minister Patrocinio González Blanco Garrido is fired by Mexican President Carlos Salinas de Gortari for allegedly downplaying the threat posed by the guerrillas.

96 La Reforma (Reform) was a period halfway through the 19th century in the history of Mexico that was characterized by liberal reforms designed to modernize Mexico and make it into a nation state. The major goals in this movement were: Land reform—redistribution

of land, separation of church and state, and increased educational opportunities for the poor, the majority of the country's population. The liberals' strategy was to sharply limit the traditional privileges land holdings of the Catholic Church and thereby revitalize the market in land. The Church fought back and the gains were limited. No class of small peasants identified with the Liberal program [that] emerged, but many merchants acquired land (and tenant farmers). Many existing landowners expanded their holdings at peasant expense, and some upwardly mobile ranch owners, often mestizos, acquired land.

97 Before the 1910 Mexican Revolution that overthrew Porfirio Díaz, most of the land was owned by a single elite ruling class. Legally there was no slavery or serfdom; however, those with heavy debts, Indian wage workers, or peasants, were essentially debt-slaves to the landowners. A small percentage of rich landowners owned most of the country's farm land. With so many people brutally suppressed, revolts and revolution were common in Mexico. To relieve the Mexican peasant's plight and stabilize the country, various leaders tried different types of agrarian land reform.

President Lázaro Cárdenas passed the 1934 Agrarian Code and accelerated the pace of land reform. He helped redistribute 45,000,000 acres (180,000 km²) of land, 4,000,000 acres (16,000 km²) of which were expropriated from American owned agricultural property. This caused conflict between Mexico and the United States. Cárdenas employed tactics of noncompliance and deception to gain leverage in this international dispute.

Agrarian reform had come close to extinction in the early 1930's. The first few years of the Cárdenas' reform were marked by high food prices, falling wages, high inflation, and low agricultural yields. In 1935 land reform began sweeping across the country in the periphery and core of commercial agriculture. The Cárdenas alliance with peasant groups was awarded by the destruction of the hacienda system. Cárdenas distributed more land than all his revolutionary predecessors put together, a 400% increase. The land reform justified itself in terms of productivity; average agricultural production during the three-year period from 1939 to 1941 was higher than it had been at any time since the beginning of the revolution.

98 Mexican Independence Day

99 Mexican slang term for an AK-47; "cuernos de chivo," whose literal meaning is "goat's horns," is a reference to the curved magazine clip or banana clip that the armament uses.

100 La Comisión Nacional de los Derechos Humanos (CNDH): National Commision of Human Rights.

101 On Tuesday, the Army scours the Lacandon Jungle in search of EZLN headquarters. The number of deaths is officially estimated at 200 total—soldiers, rebels and civilians. 1,000 more are reported wounded.

102 Allusion to Ramón López Velarde's "El retorno maléfico." Author of *Zozobra* (1919), Ramón López Velarde (June 15, 1888-June 19, 1921) was a Mexican poet. His work is generally considered to be postmodern, but is unique for its subject matter. He achieved great fame in his native land, to the point of being considered Mexico's national poet.

103 Sometimes referred to as "Easter candle."

104 Flame trees are also known as royal poincianas; "Ligustrum lucidum" (Glossy Privet, Chinese Privet or Broad-leaf Privet)

105 John Lloyd Stephens (November 28, 1805-October 13, 1852) was an American explorer, writer, and diplomat. Stephens was a pivotal figure in the rediscovery of Maya civilization throughout Central America and in the planning of the Panama railroad. Author of *Incidents of Travel in Central America, Chiapas and Yucatán, Vols. 1 & 2* (1841).

106 Allusion to Rubén Darío's line "Un vulgo errante, municipal y espeso," from the poem "Soneto autumnal al Marqués de Bradomín" ("Autumn Sonnet to the Marquis of Bradomín"), from the book *Cantos de vida y esperanza* (1905); *Songs of Life and Hope*, Will Derusha and Alberto Acereda, translators, dedicated by Darío to the Spanish Generation of '98 novelist and playwright Ramón del Valle-Inclán (1866-1936). Félix Rubén García Sarmiento (January 18, 1867—February 6, 1916), known as Rubén Darío, was a Nicaraguan poet who initiated the Spanish-American literary movement known as modernismo (modernism) that flourished at the end of the 19th century. Darío has had a great and lasting influence on 20th-century Spanish literature and journalism. He has been praised as the "Prince of Castilian Letters" and undisputed father of the modernismo literary movement.

107 On Wednesday, Efraín Bartolomé makes his final diary entry. The Mexican government declares a unilateral cease-fire. The Army forced the Zapatista troops to withdraw from the centers of population, and retreat toward the jungle. Radio stations report that the Army has opened up the roads to Ocosingo: replenishments are on the way. Things are apparently returning to normal. Ambulances and medicine arrive. Electricity is restored.

108 12 January 1994: former Mexico City mayor and federal Environment Minister Manuel Camacho Solís comes to Ocosingo as government peace spokesman.

109 One of several inedible wild Mexican yams (*Dioscorea mexicana* and *Dioscorea composita*) from which progesterone can be synthesized.

110 Author's note: It's true that the Cataratas de Agua Azul (Spanish for "Blue-Water Falls") are found in the Mexican state of Chiapas. They are located in the Municipality of Tumbalá, 69 kilometers from Palenque by the road that leads towards San Cristóbal de las Casas. However, Armando Torres is referring to a much smaller waterfall in Ocosingo's second valley.

111 Doña Celina Bartolomé, the author's mother.

112 Although Plácido Flores is a very dark-skinned indigenous person, not an Afro-Mexican, it's worthwhile noting that "Afro-Mexicans are an ethnic group which exists in certain parts of Mexico such as the Costa Chica of Oaxaca and Guerrero, Veracruz and in some towns in northern Mexico. The existence of blacks in Mexico is unknown, denied or diminished in both Mexico and abroad for a number of reasons: their small numbers, heavy intermarriage with other ethnic groups and Mexico's tradition of defining itself as a "mestizaje" or mixing of European and indigenous. Mexico did have an active slave trade since the early colonial period but from the beginning, intermarriage and mixed race offspring created an elaborate caste system. This system broke down in the very late colonial period and after Independence the legal notion of race was eliminated. The creation of a national Mexican identity, especially after the Mexican Revolution, emphasized Mexico's indigenous and European past actively or passively eliminating its African one from popular consciousness.

113 The bishop of Chiapas, Samuel Ruíz, was an early convert to Liberation Theology, and the lay catechists his diocese recruited in the area where the Zapatista rebellion broke out sympathized with the emerging armed movement.

114 The Tzeltal are a North American Indian ethnic group concentrated in the central highlands of the State of Chiapas, Mexico. The Tzeltal and Tzotzil languages form the Tzeltalan subdivision of the Mayan language family.
The Tzeltal-speaking population is distributed through 12 municipios, with 13 main communities. Of the latter, 9 are almost entirely Indian (i.e., reported to be over 85 percent Tzeltal-speaking): Aguacatenango, Amatenango, Cancuc, Chanal, Chilon, Oxchuc, Tenejapa, Petalcingo, and Sitala. The other 4 communities are about 65 to 80 percent Tzeltal-speaking: Altamirano, Ocosingo, Villa de las Rosas, and Yajalón.

115 Palenque was a Maya city-state in southern Mexico that flourished in the 7th century. The Palenque ruins date back to 100 BC to its fall around 800 AD. After its decline it was absorbed into the

jungle... but has been excavated and restored and is now a famous archaeological site attracting thousands of visitors.

116 *Pinole* is a Spanish translation of the Aztec word for a coarse flour made from ground toasted maize kernels, often in a mixture with a variety of herbs and ground seeds, which can be eaten by itself or be used as the base for a beverage. The mixture is sometimes beaten with water to make a hot or cold beverage (also called pinole), or sometimes cooked.

117 *Memela*, in Chiapas and in the rest of Mexico, is a kind of corn tortilla, thick, generally round although it can be slightly oval-shaped, about 4-5 inches in size. They are cooked on a griddle, and sometimes seasoned with butter and salt. They're not folded like normal tortillas. The meal from which they're made may sometimes contain bits of bean.

118 Author's note: The minimum wage in Mexico City, which usually had higher salaries, was $1.50 per day; during the 1930's, when the ranch in question was constructed, the exchange rate was 3.60 pesos to the dollar.

119 National Autonomous University of Mexico.

120 Author's note: "dairy cattle are uncommon in tropical regions."

121 Partido Socialista de los Trabajadores: Socialist Workers Party.

122 "... indigenous communities of the selva [formed to organize] unions that could better present their demands to the state government. Their creation of the union Quiptic ta Lecubtesel laid the foundations for the uniting of numerous smaller organizations into the first nongovernmental Chiapan supraregional organization, the Asociación Rural de Interéses Colectivo (ARIC), commonly known as the 'Union of Unions.'" Nicholas Paul Higgins: *Understanding the Chiapas Rebellion: Modernist Visions and the Invisible Indian*.

123 "One indigenous organization that also grew in Chiapas during the 1980s is the National Coordinator of Indian Peoples (*Coordinadora Nacional de Pueblos Indígenas*) or CNPI." —Lynn Stephen: *Zapata Lives!: Histories and Cultural Politics in Southern Mexico*.

124 Emiliano Zapata Campesino Organization.

125 SAGARPA (Secretaria de Agricultura, Ganaderia, Desarrollo Rural, Pesca y Alimentación): Ministry of Agriculture, Livestock, Rural Development, Fishing and Nutrition.

ABOUT THE AUTHOR

EFRAÍN BARTOLOMÉ, born 1950 in Ocosingo, State of Chiapas, Mexico, is an internationally recognized poet and prize-winning environmental activist. His verses have been collected in the following volumes: *Agua lustral* (*Holy Water: Poems, 1982-1987*); *Oficio: arder* (*Poet Afire: Poems, 1982-1997*); and *El ser que somos* (*Being Who We Are*). Winner: Mexico City Prize; Aguascalientes National Poetry Award (1984); Carlos Pellicer Prize for published work (1992); Gilberto Owen National Literary Prize (1993); Jaime Sabines International Poetry Prize (1996). The Mexican government awarded him the National Forest and Wildlife Merit Prize. In 1998 he received the Chiapas Arts Prize. In 2001 he received the International Latino Arts Award in the United States. He is a member of the National Council of Creative Artists. His poems have been translated into English, French, Portuguese, Italian, German, Arabic, Galician, Nahuatl, Peninsular Mayan, and Esperanto. He works as a psychotherapist in Mexico City. Ocosingo was his first published book-length work in prose.

ABOUT THE TRANSLATOR

KEVIN BROWN, born 1960 in Kansas City, Missouri, is a biographer, essayist and translator. He is author of the biographies *Romare Bearden: Artist* (1994) and *Malcolm X: His Life and Legacy* (1995). He was a contributing editor to *The New York Public Library African-American Desk Reference* (2000). Brown's articles, essays, interviews, reviews and translations from Spanish into English have appeared in *Afterimage, Apuntes, Asymptote, The Brooklyn Rail, eXchanges, Hayden's Ferry Review, KiN, The Kansas City Star, Kirkus,* the *London Times Literary Supplement, Mayday, Metamorphoses, The Nation, Ozone Park, Review of Latin American Studies, Threepenny Review, Two Lines,* and the *Washington Post Bookworld.*

He is working on his first collection of essays.

*Calypso Editions is an artist-run,
cooperative press dedicated to publishing
quality literary books of poetry and
fiction with a global perspective. We
believe that literature is essential to
building an international community of
readers and writers and that, in a world
of digital saturation, books can serve as
physical artifacts of beauty and wonder.*

CALYPSO EDITIONS

INFO@CALYPSOEDITIONS.ORG | WWW.CALYPSOEDITIONS.ORG

Poetry in Translation
CALYPSO EDITIONS
www.CalypsoEditions.org

Athanor & Other Pohems
by Gellu Naum
Translated by MARGENTO
and Martin Woodside
Poetry, Bilingual edition
ISBN-13: 978-0-9830999-7-0

Froth: Poems
by Jarosław Mikołajewski
Translated by Piotr Florczyk
Poetry, Bilingual edition
ISBN-13: 978-0-9830999-9-4

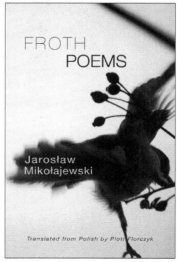

"Calypso Editions looks like a press worth paying attention to."
—Chad W. Post, *Three Percent*

Poetry
CALYPSO EDITIONS
www.CalypsoEditions.org

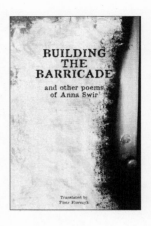

Building the Barricade
and Other Poems of Anna Swir
Poetry, Bilingual edition
Translated by Piotr Florczyk
ISBN-13: 978-0-9830999-1-8

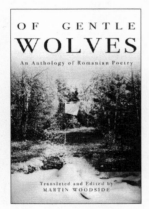

Of Gentle Wolves:
an Anthology of Romanian Poetry
Translated & Edited
by Martin Woodside
Poetry, Bilingual edition
ISBN-13: 978-0-9830999-2-5

The Vanishings
and Other Poems
by Elizabeth Myhr
Poetry
ISBN-13: 978-0-9830999-1-8

Original Titles
CALYPSO EDITIONS
www.CalypsoEditions.org

City that Ripens on the
Tree of the World
by Robin Davidson
Poetry
ISBN-13: 978-0-9887903-0-8

Use
by Derick Burleson
Poetry
ISBN-13: 978-0-9830999-5-6

The Moonflower King
by Anthony Bonds
Fiction
ISBN-13: 978-0-9830999-4-9

The Masters
CALYPSO EDITIONS
www.CalypsoEditions.org

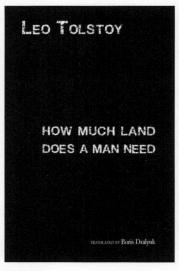

How Much Land
Does a Man Need
by Leo Tolstoy
Translated by Boris Dralyuk
Fiction, Bilingual edition
ISBN-13: 978-0-9830999-0-1

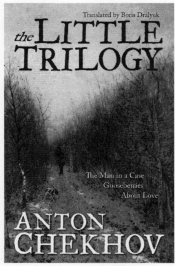

The Little Trilogy
by Anton Chekhov
Translated by Boris Dralyuk
Fiction, Bilingual edition
ISBN-13: 978-0-9887903-1-5

FOR OUR CURRENT CATALOG OF POETRY, FICTION,
AND TRANSLATION, VISIT:
www.calypsoeditions.org/free-sampler-catalog